AN
INTRODUCTION TO
ENGLISH STUDIES

Second Edition

R. L. BRETT
G. F. Grant Professor of English, University of Hull

EDWARD ARNOLD

Printed in Great Britain by
Unwin Brothers Limited
The Gresham Press Old Woking Surrey England
A member of the Staples Printing Group

Foreword

The aim of this little book is to provide a short introduction to English studies for students in upper forms of school and for those starting courses at Universities and Colleges. It makes no great claim to originality, but I have tried to bring together within a small compass the kind of information which is necessary for those embarking on a study of English at this level and which, in my experience, many students lack.

There is often a tendency in the teaching of literature to concentrate on critical judgements rather than facts. At its worst this has encouraged the student to accept *ex cathedra* judgements about literature, instead of helping him to form his own opinions. But even when the student is allowed to make up his own mind, it is important that he should know what it is that he is judging. At present we have an abundance of critical opinions and too little knowledge of the facts. If, as I believe, fact and value are inseparable, knowledge (even of the basic kind presented here) is an indispensable preliminary to critical sensibility.

Each chapter gives a list of books for further reading, and a select glossary of literary terms not covered in the text is provided in an Appendix. Many of the illustrations used in the book are taken from Gerard Manley Hopkins's *The Wreck of the Deutschland*, and for convenience of reference the text of the poem is reprinted in a second Appendix.

I should like to thank Professor Garnet Rees, who read the typescript, and Mr D. J. Palmer, who kindly checked the proofs of the original edition. The present edition has been revised and brought up to date to take account of recent publications, and the chapter on literary criticism, especially, has been considerably extended.

R. L. BRETT

Acknowledgements

Acknowledgements for permission to reproduce copyright poems are due to the following: Chatto & Windus Ltd for an extract from 'Strange Meeting' from *Poems* by Wilfred Owen; Faber & Faber Ltd for extracts from 'Burnt Norton', 'East Coker' and 'Little Gidding' from *Four Quartets*, 'The Love Song of J. Alfred Prufrock' from *Collected Poems 1909–1962*, and *The Use of Poetry and the Use of Criticism* by T. S. Eliot; Macmillan Company, New York, for an extract from 'General William Booth enters Into Heaven' from *Collected Poems* by Vachel Lindsay (1922); Oxford University Press for 'The Wreck of the Deutschland' from *Poems of Gerard Manley Hopkins*; Macmillan & Co. Ltd, New York, and the Trustees of the Hardy Estate for 'The Shadow on the Stone'.

Contents

		PAGE
1	LANGUAGE AS A LITERARY MEDIUM	1
2	THE CHIEF LITERARY FORMS: EPIC, MOCK-EPIC, TRAGEDY, COMEDY, THE NOVEL	8
3	FIGURES OF MEANING: IMAGE, METAPHOR AND SIMILE, PERSONIFICATION, SYMBOL AND MYTH	21
4	FURTHER FIGURES OF MEANING: ANTITHESIS, PARADOX AND IRONY	35
5	FIGURES OF SOUND: RHYME, ALLITERATION, ASSONANCE AND CONSONANCE	42
6	THE ELEMENTS OF PROSODY	48
7	SOME HINTS ON STYLE	57
8	A NOTE ON LITERARY CRITICISM	63
Appendix A.	A SELECT GLOSSARY OF LITERARY TERMS	70
Appendix B.	*The Wreck of the Deutschland*	76
Index		87

CHAPTER ONE

Language as a Literary Medium

In *The History of the Royal Society*, published in 1667, Thomas Sprat writes with great invective against the dangers of figurative language when used by scientists and others engaged in the search for truth. 'Who can behold without indignation', he asks, 'how many mists and uncertainties these specious *Tropes* and *Figures* have brought on our knowledge?' The members of the Royal Society, he tells us, were determined to avoid these dangers.

> They have therefore [he proceeds] been most rigorous in putting in execution the only Remedy that can be found for this *extravagance*, and that has been a constant Resolution to reject all amplifications, digressions, and swellings of style; . . . They have exacted from all their members a close, naked, natural way of speaking, positive expressions, clear senses, a native easiness, bringing all things as near the Mathematical plainness as they can . . .[1]

This division of language into a literary medium, on the one hand, designed simply to give aesthetic pleasure, and, on the other, a logical form of discourse which is concerned with the truth, has been popularized in our own day by I. A. Richards. Richards believes that there are two kinds of language. One is what he calls referential and consists of statements that are true or false, the other is emotive and expresses or evokes feeling. 'In its use of words poetry', he declares, 'is just the reverse of science.' Literature, and especially poetry, according to Richards, does not express thought but emotion. 'Misunderstanding and under-estimation of poetry,' he writes, 'is mainly due to over-estimation

[1] *Critical Essays of the Seventeenth Century*, ed. J. E. Spingarn, 1908, II, pp. 117–18.

of the thought in it. . . . It is never what a poem *says* which matters, but what it *is*.' [1]

It is doubtful whether this neat division of language into two quite distinct kinds will really stand up to examination. In the first place, plain scientific or discursive prose (*i.e.* prose which has a logical structure) is not nearly so plain when one comes to analyse it. The scientist, like all of us, has recourse to figures of speech when he tries to make his meaning clear. Phrases such as 'the Universe is *running down*', 'the specimen is *bombarded* with neutrons', and 'the super-ego acts as a *censor* of the thoughts which emerge from the unconscious', all depend upon concealed imagery. This is not to argue that the scientist is wrong to use such phrases, but it illustrates the dependence of all language upon metaphor, simile, analogy and other figures, in its constant attempt to say something significant.

But Richards is right when he insists that poetry (and indeed all forms of literature) is a *making*. The very name *poetry* means 'making' in Greek, and the Greek word *poiema* (work of art) has traditionally been distinguished from *logos* (logical discourse). The relationship between *poiema* and *logos* has been the subject of debate from classical times to our own day. Plato attacked both poetry and rhetoric as deceitful and banished poets from his ideal Republic as liars, who might mislead the people in morals and religion. His pupil Aristotle wrote two treatises, the *Rhetoric* and the *Poetics*, to answer these charges. He defended rhetoric on the ground that some people are unmoved by an appeal only to reason and he argued that rhetorical devices could be brought to the aid of reason. Rhetoric as an art of persuasion is legitimate when used with the right motives. As employed by a Hitler it could be a dangerous weapon, but how essential then to have a Winston Churchill who could beat him at his own game. Poetry, too, according to Aristotle, is not an enemy of morality but its ally. It provides an outlet for emotions which might become dangerous if they were repressed and sets before us examples of

[1] *Science and Poetry*, 1929, Ch. II.

virtue and nobility. It provides a vision of things not as they are, but as they ought to be.

Aristotle's teaching became the basis of English critical theory during the Renaissance and was crystallized in the view that literature has the twofold rôle of pleasing and instructing. It pleases because it unifies the writer's experience into an artistic pattern, and it instructs because it holds up to men a vision of a golden world which transcends the moral deficiencies of actual human history. The instruction and the pleasure are two aspects of a single whole; the work of art pleases by instructing and instructs by pleasing.

Even at the time of the Renaissance there were elements in English critical theory which hinted at a more profound relationship between *poiema* and *logos* than Aristotle had elaborated. But it was not until the Romantic Revival that these were fully developed. The English critic, above all others, to whom we owe the first really philosophical analysis of this relationship was Coleridge. Even Coleridge never produced a comprehensive theory of literature, but in his *Biographia Literaria* and other writings, we are given an outline of a new poetics. In contradistinction to I. A. Richards, Coleridge believed that *poiema* and *logos* are not separate, but that there is an interplay between them by which the human mind thinks and expresses itself. For him poetry is a symbolic structure. The poet creates a set of symbols which are more than an expression of the poet's feelings; poetry symbolizes thought of a kind which can be expressed in no other way. As he declares in *Biographia Literaria*, 'An idea, in the highest sense of that word, cannot be conveyed but by a *symbol*.'[1] It is true that Coleridge contrasts poetry and science when he writes, 'A poem is that species of composition, which is opposed to works of science, by proposing for its *immediate* object pleasure, not truth.'[2] But the important qualification here is in the word 'immediate'. A poem—and the same is true of all works of literature—will give the reader pleasure; this is its initial aim. It

[1] op. cit., Ch. IX.   [2] ibid., Ch. XIV.

will delight us by the artistic control of its material, by its pattern and shape. But it does more than this. It will stir the mind to reflection and speculation. There is thus a constant interplay between imaginative creation and conceptual thinking. The intellect will feed the imagination and the imagination will stimulate the intellect. The artistic imagination, then, has a vital function in our thinking and Coleridge describes it as 'the agent of the reason'.

What Coleridge meant can be illustrated at a simple level by the first stanza of Gerard Manley Hopkins's *The Wreck of the Deutschland* (*Appendix B*). An attempt at paraphrasing this stanza would run something like this. God, who is the Creator and sustainer of all things, is concerned with the life of every individual. This concern expresses itself in ways which defy our understanding and God's love will appear to us at times as terrifying and destructive. This is the theme of the whole poem, which recounts the death by drowning of five nuns who had been exiled from their fatherland by an act of intolerant legislation. What appears to be a tragedy is, to the believer, part of God's loving purpose, a re-enactment of the Crucifixion which, because of the Resurrection, turns tragedy into comedy, that is, something with a happy ending. The opening stanza introduces this great theme by a series of symbols: *breath* (life itself), *bread* (the means of sustaining life), *strand* and *sea* (the world of nature), *bones*, *veins* and *flesh* (the individual), *finger* (God's concern for the individual, which we feel sometimes with terror, because we would sooner be left alone). The second stanza develops this sense of terror with the symbols of *lightning* and *lashed rod*, which strike us down and yet paradoxically are the instruments of God's love. Even in these stanzas—and more so in the whole poem, of course—we perceive two main characteristics of literary language. The first of these is the sheer pleasure we are given by the brilliant manipulation of words in the pattern Hopkins adopts. The second is the realization that he is saying something that could not be said so exactly in any other way. The literary form and the meaning are inseparable. The meaning could be expressed, though less adequately, in theological language, and no doubt theology helped the poet towards the belief he expresses here. In other words, *logos* has helped and inspired *poiema*. But the intensely personal conviction that pervades these stanzas and dictates their form must also assist theology, which is an endeavour to express religious experience in logical statements. And so *poiema* revitalizes *logos*.

A work of literature, therefore, not only *is*, but also *says* something. What it says will never be precise in the way that logical propositions are precise, but it is not therefore without meaning. If asked to define the meaning of, say, *King Lear*, we could hardly put it in the form of propositions like 'filial piety is a desirable quality', 'inflexibility of mind is likely to lead to family difficulties', 'love discloses itself in action not words', and so on. In fact there is no adequate paraphrase, no substitute, for the play itself. The play carries its own meaning, which can only be approximated by attempts at paraphrase. What it *says* and what it *is* are inseparable. But this does not rule out the possibility of commentary *about* the play, and the job of both the critic and the scholar is to reveal its meaning more clearly. The job is never-ending, for the meaning of a great work of art is inexhaustible.

The creation of literature often involves an immensely more subtle and complicated use of language than does discursive prose. This is true not only of poetry but of all literature, though verse employs devices of its own, such as metre and rhyme, and is readier to defy the conventions of syntax than prose. Literary language has these characteristics because it is a symbolic structure. The word *symbol* suggests a holding together, and literary language very often holds together several meanings in one symbol or set of symbols. *Ambiguity* has become a fashionable term in modern criticism, but the notion that a literary work carries a multiplicity of meanings is no more than traditional.

The richness, the ambiguity, and the defiance of syntax, can all be illustrated in one line of *The Wreck of the Deutschland*, the last line of stanza twenty-four. The drowning nun calls to Christ in her agony:

> The cross to her she calls Christ to her,

By giving this sentence a double object (*cross* and *Christ*), Hopkins with a great compression of language indicates that her salvation will come in the form of death. There is a tremendous concentration of meaning as well as language in this sentence. The remainder of the line is equally compact:

> christens her wild-worst Best.

For the Christian, the Crucifixion was at once the worst possible event in history and yet at the same time the best. In crucifying the Son of God, man perpetrated the worst crime of which he was capable and yet in doing so he paradoxically made possible his own salvation. So for the nun, her terrible death is also her greatest good. Her *wild-worst* death becomes her *Best*, her union with God. But this is so only to the believer and Hopkins indicates this by the key-word *christens*. The profession of faith which the Christian makes, or which is made for him, at baptism, enables him to see death not as the end but as the beginning, not as a curse but as a blessing.

A simple example of condensed syntax is seen in the first lines of stanza seventeen of Hopkins's poem:

> They fought with God's cold —
> And they could not and fell to the deck
> (Crushed them) or water (and drowned them) or rolled
> With the sea-romp over the wreck.

But literary language is not always so condensed. It sometimes uses simple and direct statement, as in the first line of stanza twelve—'On Saturday sailed from Bremen'—where we find the brevity and 'telegraphese' of the newspaper headline. In fact, literature will use language in every way it can, conventionally or experimentally, with the widest range of effects that words can be forced to yield. The following chapters will describe some of the means by which it does this in its attempt to achieve a linguistic pattern that is both meaningful and aesthetically moving. The chapter on literary criticism also deals with the question of how far the study of stylistics can help to throw light on the use of language in literary forms.

For Further Reading

I. A. Richards, *Principles of Literary Criticism*, 1924.
D. Davie, *Articulate Energy*, 1955.
R. L. Brett, *Reason and Imagination*, 1960.
Winifred Nowottny, *The Language Poets Use*, 1962.

CHAPTER TWO

The Chief Literary Forms
Epic, Mock-Epic, Tragedy, Comedy, The Novel

Traditionally there have been certain fixed forms or 'kinds' (*genres*) by which the literary artist has given his work pattern. The importance of these has declined in the last two centuries and we have seen literary works which do not belong firmly to any one 'kind'. Since the Romantic Revival the conviction has gathered strength that content should govern form and that every literary work determines its own shape. But these traditional forms were not imposed arbitrarily upon the writer, and literature by the very nature of its material still tends to be influenced by them. To understand and appreciate literature, especially the literature of the past, we need to know something of the main *genres* within which the writer has worked. The following are the chief ones; for information on the minor forms the reader should consult the *Select Glossary of Literary Terms* (*Appendix A*).

The Epic

Another name for the epic is the *heroic poem* and one of its chief characteristics is that it tells the story of a hero whose exploits have a national significance. It is a long, narrative poem written in an elevated style. There are two kinds of epic, the *primary* and the *secondary*. The primary epic developed from ancient legend and recounts the exploits of some great warrior who helped his country to victory. Homer's *Iliad* and *Odyssey* are the best known examples of this form and served as models for later writers. In English the Anglo-Saxon *Beowulf* belongs to this class, though its hero is not a national figure. The secondary epic appeared at a much later stage of society and was written with far greater literary sophistication by poets who imitated the primary epic. Virgil's *Æneid*, and in our own language, Milton's *Paradise Lost*, are examples of the secondary epic. In his *Poetics*, Aristotle placed the epic below tragedy as a literary form, but at the Renaissance it was regarded as the supreme test of the poet's art. Certainly it is a tremendous challenge to the poet's skill and there are only a few great epics in the whole of Western literature.

The epic hero, then, is often a great national figure, and in *Paradise Lost*, Adam is the father of the entire human race. The action of the epic is on a vast scale. In the *Odyssey* it covers the events of the Trojan War and the wanderings of Odysseus on his way home from the war. In *Paradise Lost* it moves between Heaven, Hell and Earth. The hero is more than simply human, for his fate and the fate of his nation are the concern of the gods or God. Heaven intervenes in his affairs by means of divine agents, either minor gods or angels, who are referred to as the epic *machinery*.

The style of the epic is elevated to suit its high theme. In *Paradise Lost* Milton elaborated a style which has been regarded by some critics, especially Johnson, T. S. Eliot and F. R. Leavis, as artificial in a bad sense. But the style of *Paradise Lost* is ideally suited for its purpose. It has what De Quincey called 'an interplanetary wheeling' which matches the cosmic action, and its tight Latinate syntax and dropping of the numerous particles that encumber normal English, make it an ideal vehicle for carrying the narrative forward over twelve books. One of the features of the epic style is the long simile. An example of this is to be found in Book I of *Paradise Lost* where Satan, after his banishment from Heaven, is seen lying on the burning lake in Chaos.

> Thus Satan talking to his neerest Mate
> With Head up-lift above the wave, and Eyes
> That sparkling blaz'd; his other Parts besides
> Prone on the Flood, extended long and large
> Lay floating many a rood, in bulk as huge

As whom the Fables name of monstrous size,
. . . . . .
. . . . or that Sea-beast
Leviathan, which God of all his works
Created hugest that swim th' Ocean stream!
Him haply slumbring on the *Norway* foam
The Pilot of some small night-founderd Skiff,
Deeming some Iland, oft, as Sea-men tell,
With fixed Anchor in his skaly rinde
Moors by his side under the Lee, while Night
Invests the Sea, and wished Morn delayes:
So stretcht out huge in length the Arch-fiend lay
Chaind on the burning lake.

The procedure the epic poet adopts is generally to state the theme of his poem—*Paradise Lost* starts, 'Of Mans First Dis-obedience', etc.—to invoke the heavenly Muse to assist him in his task, and then to plunge into the middle of his narrative (*in medias res*). The beginning of the action is told in retrospect and sometimes its ultimate conclusion foretold at the end of the poem. So *Paradise Lost* begins with Satan and his followers already in Hell, and the events which led to their Fall from Heaven are re-lated to Adam by Raphael much later in the poem. Similarly, at the end of the poem, Michael recounts to Adam the chief epi-sodes of Old Testament history which lead up to the coming of Christ, the second Adam who will heal the breach between man-kind and God.

The Wreck of the Deutschland is an elegy and not an epic, but it has certain features that relate it to epic. It starts with a statement of the theme, there is something like an invocation to God to assist the poet in his task, there is the story of the heroic nun, the battle with the sea, celestial 'machines', which here are the ele-ments themselves, and an anticipation of the results of the action in a stirring of 'English souls' towards God.

The Mock-Epic

The *mock-epic* is a poetic form which uses the epic structure but on a miniature scale and with a subject that is mean or trivial. Its purpose is satirical; to make the subject look ridiculous by placing it in a framework entirely inappropriate to its importance. At the end of the seventeenth century, scientific modes of thinking made it increasingly difficult to write epic, which depends upon a mythological framework and the use of heavenly 'machinery'. In some ways *Paradise Lost* was a *tour de force* and Milton achieved his success against great difficulties. Dryden satisfied his poetic ambitions by combining the epic and satire. Both *Absalom and Achitophel* (1681) and *MacFlecknoe* (1682) have epic features, though written on a much smaller scale than real epic. But the best known and most brilliant example of the form came a little later in Pope's *The Rape of the Lock* (1712). The central incident in the poem is the theft of a lock of hair and the ensuing quarrel between two families. All the main features of epic surround this incident. The style is elevated, there is celestial 'machinery' in the form of the sylphs, a voyage (though only in Belinda's barge on the Thames), a visit to the underworld and battles (though one is only at cards). By placing this incident in such a framework, Pope hoped to show the 'rape' as trivial and so to reconcile the two families. He failed in this purpose, but he has given lasting pleasure to his readers ever since. (*v.* under **Irony** in Chapter 4.)

For Further Reading

C. M. Bowra, *From Virgil to Milton*, 1945.
E. M. W. Tillyard, *The English Epic and its Background*, 1954.
C. S. Lewis, *Preface to Paradise Lost*, 1941.
J. S. Cunningham, *Pope: The Rape of the Lock*, 1961.
Paul Merchant, *The Epic* (Critical Idiom Series), 1971.
J. D. Jump, *Burlesque* (Critical Idiom Series), 1972.

Tragedy

The term tragedy is generally reserved for drama, but the

novel (see below) has taken over tragic as well as epic subjects and is parasitic upon these and other forms. The chief statement of the nature of tragedy is to be found in Aristotle's *Poetics*, which was written over two thousand years ago. It is as well to remember that Aristotle was not laying down *a priori* rules which should govern tragedy for all time, but reflecting on the great age of Greek tragedy of the time of Aeschylus, Sophocles and Euripides and endeavouring to discern the principles behind their work. Moreover, his treatise is incomplete and probably represents no more than notes of the lectures he gave to his students at the Lyceum in Athens. But although his observations may not have universal validity and although other types of tragedy different from the Greek have been evolved, the *Poetics* remains the most profound treatment of the subject.

Aristotle defined tragedy as 'the imitation [*i.e.* representation] of an action that is serious [*i.e.* significant], complete, of a certain magnitude, dramatically presented rather than in narrative form; through pity and fear effecting the purgation of these emotions' (*Poetics*, Ch. VI). The word imitation (*mimesis*) was probably used by Aristotle because Plato had accused the artist of imitating the world of the senses, which Plato believed to be only a copy of the Ideas or Forms behind sensory experience. Aristotle's treatise is in many ways a reply to Plato and he adopts the same word as Plato but invests it with a new meaning. *Mimesis* as used by Aristotle is better translated as 'representation' than 'copying'. The adjective 'serious' implies that the story should not be trivial but should concern itself with significant events. 'Complete, of a certain magnitude' means that the action must not be a series of un-related incidents and should be concentrated into a period that can be conveniently presented on the stage. Like epic, tragedy traditionally begins *in medias res*. The notion grew up at the time of the Renaissance that this unity of action also implied unity of time and place; that the action should be in one place and should last no longer than one day. Aristotle does refer in passing to the practice of some Greek dramatists who confined the action of their plays to twenty-four hours, but the unities of time and place are not part of his theory and belong to the neo-classicism of the seventeenth and eighteenth centuries.

The word purgation (*katharsis*) was taken from medicine and by this metaphor Aristotle was referring to what some people mean when they say they go to the cinema to have a good cry and feel all the better for it. In advancing this theory of *katharsis*, Aristotle was answering the charges made against the drama by Plato, who alleged that watching violence and wickedness on the stage would encourage these qualities in the audience. This debate has continued to our own day and we meet it in the arguments about the relation of television to juvenile delinquency. Where Aristotle seems to be unquestionably right is in his contention that witnessing events, which in real life would produce horror and pain, in dramatic form gives us relief and even pleasure. But though Aristotle believed *katharsis* to be a product of tragedy, he did not consider this to be its end. The purpose of tragedy, he argued, is intelligent pleasure.

Tragedy, like epic, is centred upon a hero. In Aristotle's account this hero should be neither wholly good nor wholly bad. The one would make his tragic fate intolerable for us, the other would remove him from our sympathy. He should be a man like ourselves, though rather better than average, and of sufficient status for his downfall to involve others as well as himself. Given these conditions, we experience pity (for we feel that his misfortunes are not entirely deserved) and terror (for we can imagine ourselves in his place). The tragic hero suffers a change in his fortunes from happiness to misery, which is produced by some fatal error of judgement (*hamartia*). The tragic error was generally attributable in Greek tragedy to overweening pride (*hubris*) which offended divine justice (*dike*). This *hubris* brought upon itself the judgement of the gods (*nemesis*). The tragic story, or plot, according to Aristotle, moved from a beginning, through complication, to a catastrophe or tragic reversal, both of intention and fortune. This reversal (*peripeteia*) becomes apparent to the audience before the hero himself is aware of it and thus produces an element of dramatic irony which is sustained until his own tragic recognition (*anagnorisis*) of the real situation.

The most famous story which illustrates this pattern is that of Oedipus, son of Laius (king of Thebes) and Jocasta. Laius, learning from an oracle that he was destined to be killed by Oedipus, exposed his child upon Mount Cithaeron. But the baby was found by a shepherd and taken to the court of Polybus, king of Corinth, who brought him up as his own son. When he was grown to manhood, Oedipus was told by the oracle of Delphi that he would kill his father and incestuously marry his mother. Thinking Polybus to be his father he left Corinth and journeying towards Thebes fell in with Laius. A quarrel ensued and Oedipus killed his father, though unaware of his identity. On arriving in Thebes he met and married his mother, by whom he had four children. On learning the truth, he blinds himself, and Jocasta commits suicide. Oedipus wanders away accompanied by his favourite daughter, Antigone, but is finally removed from the earth by the Eumenides (Furies). This story, which belonged to legend, formed the subject of some of the greatest Greek tragedies, of which the best-known is Sophocles' trilogy, *Oedipus Rex*, *Oedipus Coloneus*, and *Antigone*. It contains all the elements which Aristotle considered essential to tragedy.

Aristotle devotes a large part of the *Poetics* to a discussion of plot (*muthos*) and some critics have felt that he gives too much attention to this and too little to character. The word *muthos* means 'story' or 'fable' and Aristotle is not over-concerned with plot in the modern sense, that is, the contrivances that fit the pieces of the story together. For him, plot and character are a false antithesis, since character can be revealed only in action and character is, therefore, necessarily subordinate to plot. This accords both with Aristotle's writings on ethics, which advance the view that a man is judged by his actions, and with the practice of the great Greek tragic dramatists, who were interested not so much in the analysis of motives as in telling a tragic story in which characters played their parts.

Although Aristotle became the great philosopher for the schoolmen of the Middle Ages, his *Poetics* was unknown until a Latin translation appeared in 1498. By the middle of the sixteenth century, however, its influence and authority were well recognized. But it was by no means the only force that shaped the tragedy of the Elizabethan period, which produced the greatest dramatic tragedies in English literature. Elizabethan tragedy owed much to the Miracle and Morality plays of the Middle Ages (*v. Appendix A*), and another important influence was the Roman writer, Seneca.

Senecan tragedy led to two developments. One of these was the full five-act drama in a neo-classical manner, with an observance of the unities of time and place, a chorus, and a high-flown style, but with much more rhetoric than action. An example of this kind of play is Sackville and Norton's *Gorboduc* (1562). The other development was the tremendous popularity of the revenge tragedy. Revenge had been a favourite subject of Seneca's plays and the appearance of Kyd's *Spanish Tragedy* started a whole series of plays which exploited this theme and which introduced madness, murder, suicide, incest, ghosts, and other horrors. *Hamlet* owes something to this fashion, but raises these themes to a new level of tragic intensity.

Two other features differentiate English Elizabethan tragedy from the classical Greek. The first, which was inherited from medieval drama, was the mingling of comic elements with the tragic. Sometimes these elements were alien to the tragic theme, but on occasion (and one thinks especially of the Fool in *King Lear* and the grave-diggers in *Hamlet*) they increased the tragic tension by slackening it for a while, emphasizing the tragedy by a kind of counterpoint. The second feature is **tragi-comedy** which is a very English form. Here the action starts as though it will produce a tragic outcome, but the 'reversal' is a happy one, as for instance in Shakespeare's *The Winter's Tale*. Aristotle gives a place to this kind of drama in his *Poetics*, but it was never developed in Greek drama to the extent that it was by the Jacobeans.

During the Restoration period there developed a form which grafted epic on to tragedy. This is known as the **heroic drama.** The style of the heroic drama was very rhetorical. The hero was a warrior, and the theme often involved the fate of a nation. A typical subject was the conflict between love and patriotic duty, and perhaps the greatest example of the kind is Dryden's *All For Love*, which is an adaptation of Shakespeare's *Antony and Cleopatra* in this manner.

Tragedy as a dramatic form declined in the eighteenth and early nineteenth centuries, but a revival started with Ibsen, and today we have important tragic dramatists such as Synge, O'Neill, Brecht, Tennessee Williams, Arthur Miller, T. S. Eliot and Pinter, though only the last two of these are English, and only one of them (Pinter) English by birth.

For Further Reading

J. W. H. Atkins, *Literary Criticism in Antiquity*, vol. I, 1934.
F. L. Lucas, *Tragedy in Relation to Aristotle's Poetics*, 1928.
John Jones, *On Aristotle and Greek Tragedy*, 1963.
F. L. Lucas, *Seneca and Elizabethan Tragedy*, 1922.
A. C. Bradley, *Shakespearean Tragedy*, 1905.
Theodore Spencer, *Death and Elizabethan Tragedy*, 1936.
D. G. James, *The Dream of Learning*, 1951.
Cleanth Brooks (ed.), *Tragic Themes in Western Literature*, 1955.
H. D. F. Kitto, *Form and Meaning in Drama*, 1956.
J. Lawlor, *The Tragic Sense in Shakespeare*, 1960.
E. Bentley, *The Modern Theatre*, 1948.
Clifford Leech, *Tragedy* (Critical Idiom Series), 1969.
Helen Gardner, *Religion and Literature*, 1971.

Comedy

Comedy is generally the representation in dramatic form of an action that ends happily, but it has also come to mean a story, especially a play, that arouses laughter. Aristotle's treatment of comedy in his *Poetics* was lost from the text and the form never received the authority his name gave to tragedy. Comedy developed in England from the buffoonery and farce which interspersed the Miracle and Morality plays in the Middle Ages and from the influence of the Latin writers Plautus and Terence. But Shakespeare, especially, raised it to a high level and wrote comedies of various kinds. *The Comedy of Errors* is modelled on a play by Plautus, and *The Merry Wives of Windsor* approaches sheer farce, but Shakespeare's individual achievement is in romantic comedy, such as *Twelfth Night*, *As You Like It*, and *Much Ado About Nothing*, where idealized love runs its chequered career to a successful conclusion. Comedy often embraces satire, and in Ben Jonson's plays the cause of laughter is often the greediness and venality of characters who are tricked by rascals. Both the rogues and their victims are exposed for what they are, as in *The Alchemist* (1610). The dramatic action often involves a reversal of fortune, but never so serious as to become tragic. (*v. Appendix A*, under **Humour.**)

The Restoration saw the emergence of the **comedy of manners**, which is concerned with the conventions of a highly artificial society, and where the brilliance of wit and dialogue and the amusing situations sustain the sometimes rather slight story. Congreve's *The Way of the World* (1700) is perhaps the best example of this. A good deal of Restoration comedy was licentious and there was a reaction to this in the sentimental comedy of the early eighteenth century. But this type of play was often more sentimental than comic and provoked a further reaction in the work of Goldsmith and Sheridan, especially in Goldsmith's *The Good Natured Man* (1769), where a morality of sensibility is reduced to comic absurdity.

In the Victorian age there was a decline of comedy as of tragedy, but with Oscar Wilde and G. B. Shaw a revival began. But though there have been many distinguished plays written in our own day, which count as comedies, few of them are comic simply because they provoke laughter. T. S. Eliot's *The Cocktail Party* (1950) is a comedy because it moves beyond tragedy to a 'happy' view of the universe; it is comedy in the traditional sense that Dante's *Divine Comedy* is.

The most important development in drama in the present

century took place after the second world war and is often referred to as the 'theatre of the absurd'. This kind of drama, especially on the Continent, has its roots in existentialism and is best represented in the work of writers like Ionesco and Beckett. In England its chief representatives are N. F. Simpson and Harold Pinter. It is difficult to classify the 'theatre of the absurd' as comedy. Plays such as Beckett's *Waiting For Godot* (produced in London, 1955) and Pinter's *The Caretaker* (1959) certainly arouse laughter in the audience, but their overall effect—pity for the human condition and an awareness of the grotesque and terrifying aspects of experience—bring them close to tragedy.

No one has produced a systematic and philosophical account of comedy. Hobbes, in the seventeenth century, advanced a theory based upon the notion of *katharsis*, which suggested that comedy relieves our feelings in laughter when we witness someone else suffer a misfortune that might have happened to ourselves. But it is doubtful whether this matches all the complexities of the subject. Shaftesbury, in the eighteenth century, asserted that ridicule is a test of the truth, but this and similar theories, though they might cover satirical comedy, are not comprehensive enough. Meredith in *The Idea of Comedy* (1877) wrote of the comic spirit as arising from men's infringement of justice and natural law. This infringement was not so gross as to provoke tragic nemesis, but sufficient only to produce heavenly laughter. Few writers have got beyond the truth that comedy is based upon the recognition of an incongruity that strikes us as absurd.

For Further Reading

H. Bergson, *Laughter: An Essay on the Meaning of the Comic* (English trans.), 1921.

A. H. Thorndike, *English Comedy*, 1929.

L. J. Potts, *Comedy*, 1948.

J. R. Brown & B. Harris (eds), *Contemporary Theatre: Stratford-upon-Avon Studies*, 4, 1962.

Martin Esslin, *Theatre of the Absurd*, 1962.

Arnold Hinchliffe, *The Absurd* (Critical Idiom Series), 1969.

Moelwyn Merchant, *Comedy* (Critical Idiom Series), 1972.

The Novel

The novel, which was the last of the major literary forms to appear, has now become the most popular and has tended to swallow the others. It has taken over a good deal of what in earlier days would have been epic, tragedy, and comedy. The name is given to almost any extended work of prose fiction. The epic was succeeded by the romance, which whether in verse (*e.g.* Spenser's *The Faerie Queene*) or in prose (*e.g.* Malory's *Morte D'Arthur*), embodied the ideals of knightly chivalry. But as the epic and romance went out of circulation and there grew up a middle-class reading public and a cheaper form of book-production, the novel became a dominant form.

In some ways the novel started as anti-epic and anti-romance. The first great European novel was Cervantes' *Don Quixote* (1605), which is a satire on the tradition of chivalry, and though Fielding in his Preface to *Joseph Andrews* (1742) described his novel as an epic in prose, in form and subject-matter it is closer to mock-epic than epic proper. There had been prose fiction of various kinds in the sixteenth and seventeenth centuries; pastoral romances like Sir Philip Sidney's *Arcadia* (1590), the tales of Tudor apprentices by Thomas Deloney, the brief 'characters' of the seventeenth century, which depicted imaginary personalities, and the great religious allegories of Bunyan. But the first English writer to deserve the name of novelist is Daniel Defoe. Because Defoe was early on the scene and was a journalist, and since he wrote in the picaresque style (*picaro* is the Spanish word for rogue and in sixteenth-century Spain there were a number of loosely constructed stories in the manner of our own Deloney), it has often been thought that his was an amateurish beginning. In fact Defoe was a great novelist and though his plots are little more than episodic, he showed a masterly control of his material and a superb artistry in giving his narratives realism. *Robinson Crusoe* (1719), *The Journal of the Plague Year* (1722) and *Moll Flanders* (1722) have depths which escape the casual reader. Defoe was followed in the eighteenth century by Fielding (*Joseph Andrews*, 1742, and *Tom Jones*, 1749) and Richardson (*Pamela*, 1740, and *Clarissa*, 1747).

The novel reached its apotheosis in the nineteenth century and it would be impossible here to give an account of its development up to the present day. Various techniques have been employed by the novelist with a variety of purposes. There has been the epistolary novel, that is, written in the form of letters (Richardson); the quasi-autobiographical novel (Defoe and Charlotte Brontë); the allegorical novel (Kafka and George Orwell); the novel that makes use of symbolism (Dickens); the satirical novel (Thackeray); the stream-of-consciousness novel (Virginia Woolf); the novel that provides a mythic framework for depicting modern life (James Joyce); the novel that reveals the action in dialogue and has little narrative (Ivy Compton-Burnett), and so on.

For Further Reading

Percy Lubbock, *The Craft of Fiction*, 1921.
E. M. Forster, *Aspects of the Novel*, 1927.
Edwin Muir, *The Structure of the Novel*, 1928.
W. E. Allen, *The English Novel*, 1954.
Ian Watt, *The Rise of the Novel*, 1957.
Miriam Allott, *Novelists on the Novel*, 1960.
L. Stevenson, *The English Novel*, 1960.
Wayne Booth, *Rhetoric of Fiction*, 1961.
Barbara Hardy, *The Appropriate Form*, 1964.

CHAPTER THREE

Some Figures of Meaning
Image, Metaphor and Simile, Personification, Symbol and Myth

In Chapter One we discussed the literary use of language and argued that the *immediate* purpose of literature is to create a work of art which will give the reader pleasure. In Chapter Two we outlined some of the main forms that serve this purpose by giving a literary work shape. These embraced both poetry and prose, for the difference between *poiema* and *logos* is not the difference between verse and prose. A literary work is analogous to a vase, a painting or a piece of music. It gives us aesthetic pleasure because we can contemplate it as an object; we see it as a whole, just as we see a vase or painting, or retain in our memories the first notes of a musical composition while we listen to the remainder. T. S. Eliot expresses this very finely in *Burnt Norton* :

> Only by the form, the pattern,
> Can words or music reach
> The stillness, as a Chinese jar still
> Moves perpetually in its stillness,
> Not the stillness of the violin, while the note lasts,
> Not that only, but the co-existence,
> Or say that the end precedes the beginning,
> And the end and the beginning were always there
> Before the beginning and after the end.

Eliot describes here how language, which normally operates in a time sequence of words, overcomes this disadvantage in a literary form and creates an object that is almost spatially extended. Coleridge was being even more precise when he said that poetry has 'a middle quality betwixt a thought and a thing'.

We should expect literary language, then, to be much more

concrete than discursive language, and this is especially true of poetry. Poetry is quite capable of using abstractions and may, indeed, contain (as in the quotation from *Burnt Norton* above) passages of argument in discursive terms. But such abstractions serve a totality which is itself concrete. Literary language employs various devices which exploit this tendency to concreteness and the following are the more important of these. These figures of speech are often called *tropes*, though the term is sometimes extended to include all devices of rhetoric.

Image

Like most other words in literary criticism, *image* and *imagery* bear a wide range of meanings. Today they generally refer to any use of language which depends on concrete particulars rather than abstractions. The most common error is to identify imagery with mental pictures. The psychologist uses the word *image* in this way, but even in psychology *image* is not confined to vision. Each of the five senses has its own kind of image and the psychologist speaks of the olfactory image (smell), the gustatory image (taste), the auditory image (hearing), the tactile image (touch), as well as the visual image. In addition, the psychologist sometimes refers to a kinaesthetic image, which relates to our sense of movement or to our awareness of bodily effort.

Poetic imagery is rooted in sensory images of this kind, but it would be a mistake to think that we must constantly be seeing mental pictures or hearing imaginary sounds when we read poetry. Indeed, if this happened it would be a hindrance and not a help to our reading. When Donne, in *A Valediction Forbidding Mourning*, compares his mistress and himself to a pair of compasses, we are not meant to visualize the compasses. The comparison is an intellectual and not a sensory one. When T. S. Eliot writes in *Prufrock*,

> Let us go then, you and I,
> When the evening is spread out against the sky
> Like a patient etherised upon a table;

a mental picture of an operating theatre would simply be a distraction. In certain instances the image is simply one example of a whole class of which it stands as the concrete representative. When, in the same poem, Eliot writes:

> For I have known them all already, known them all:
> Have known the evenings, mornings, afternoons,
> I have measured out my life with coffee spoons;

the coffee spoons are an image of the triviality of the social round, which includes coffee-parties amongst other ephemeral pleasures. The technical name for an image of this kind is **metonym**. A good example of it is seen in Shirley's lines,

> Sceptre and crown must tumble down
> And in the dust be equal made
> With the poor crooked scythe and spade,

where *sceptre*, *crown*, *scythe* and *spade* are chosen from various insignia that represent the Court and the peasantry. In stanza one of *The Wreck of the Deutschland*, *breath* and *bread*, *bones*, *veins* and *flesh* are all examples of **synecdoche**, where the image is literally part of a whole and not merely a representative of it.

Though imagery does not necessarily create mental pictures, tastes, sounds, etc., its sensory basis often gives vividness and force to language. In stanza eight of Hopkins's poem the bittersweet quality of God's will for us is brought out in an image that almost produces a taste in the mouth:

> How a lush-kept plush-capped sloe
> Will, mouthed to flesh-burst,
> Gush!—flush the man, the being with it, sour or sweet.

In the opening lines of stanza ten,

> With an anvil-ding
> And with fire in him forge thy will,

we can almost see and hear God, as a blacksmith, hammering the intractable material of human nature into a shape conformable to his design. Stanza fourteen of the poem is full of kinaesthetic imagery so vivid that we feel buffeted and beaten with the ship herself.

Metaphor and Simile

Metaphor and simile are fundamentally the same figure of speech, the only distinction between them being a grammatical convention. The basis of both is to express one thing in terms of another. In the simile the relationship is expressed by a term such as *like* or *as*, whereas in the metaphor there is a straight identification. Thus Burns's

> O my love's like a red, red rose,

is a simile, and the line from a popular song,

> You're the cream in my coffee,

is a metaphor.

Critics traditionally have regarded the ability to create metaphors as the hall-mark of the poetic imagination. In a chapter of his *Poetics* dealing with style, Aristotle wrote: 'The greatest thing by far is to have a command of metaphor. . . . It is the sign of genius, for to make good metaphors implies an eye for resemblances.' Hobbes in his *Leviathan* argued that the imagination is the faculty which perceives similarities, whereas the judgement (or intellect) discerns differences. Coleridge, too, saw the imagination as a synthesizing process which unifies experience in images which contain a multiplicity of meanings.

Sometimes the elements in a metaphor are far-fetched or the relationship between them elaborate or artificial. The term **conceit** is often applied to such figures. Elizabethan lyric poetry was fond of conceits, and the metaphysical poets of the seventeenth century employed metaphorical language so extravagantly that Johnson, in his *Life* of Cowley, said that in their verse 'The most heterogeneous ideas are yoked by violence together'. The most notorious example of the metaphysical conceit is Crashaw's comparison in *Saint Mary Magdalene* of the Magdalene's tearful eyes to

> two faithful fountains,
> Two walking baths, two weeping motions,
> Portable and compendious oceans.

Stanza four of *The Wreck of the Deutschland* illustrates the successful use of both metaphor and simile. It begins with the comparison of the poet and an hour-glass. Like the sand in an hour-glass, the poet's thoughts and feelings lack stability; his faith is likely to crumble and run out. But as the hour-glass is fixed to the wall, so is the poet held fast to God's being. This is an objective fact, quite independent, in the one instance, of the sand's motion, and in the other, of the poet's psychological turmoil. In the middle of the stanza a complicated simile takes over from the metaphor to make the poet's meaning more exact. Here the comparison is with the water in a well, which is kept at a constant level by the pressure of the springs that feed it. A *pane* is a lock in an irrigation system that holds the water steady. The water that is fed into the well through this system comes from the surrounding hills on which the springs appear in the distance almost as ropes, motionless and solid. The word *roped* also suggests the security of the believer's attachment to God, as one climber is roped to another on the mountain face (the word *voel* is the Welsh word for hillside). The pressure of water is then compared with God's grace—'a vein of the gospel proffer' (where 'proffer' is a noun meaning 'offering'), 'a principle' (that is, a governing factor in the situation), 'Christ's gift'. The image of the hour-glass has its validity; it suggests an objective security as against a subjective insecurity. But the image of the well advances the meaning further. In spite of inner turmoil, a steadiness and tranquillity are given and sustained by God's grace.

It is often suggested that to mix one's metaphors is stylistically wrong. A famous mixed metaphor, or (to give it the correct technical name) **catachresis,** occurs in Hamlet's great soliloquy, in which he puts the question,

> Whether 'tis nobler in the mind to suffer
> The slings and arrows of outrageous fortune,
> Or, to take arms against a sea of troubles
> And by opposing end them?

The phrase 'to take arms against a sea of troubles' is undoubtedly a mixed metaphor and has led some editors to suggest that the text must be corrupt and that this is not what Shakespeare wrote. But Shakespeare is full of mixed metaphors. In one of his sonnets he writes:

> O how can summer's honey breath hold out
> Against the wreckful siege of battering days?

This is a mixed metaphor which if pressed to a literal conclusion would be ridiculous. But we must not press a metaphor to yield an exact literal meaning. The relationship between the two elements in a metaphor is not an exact one; there is a resemblance at some points, but not at every point.

For Further Reading

I. A. Richards, *Philosophy of Rhetoric*, 1936.
C. Day Lewis, *The Poetic Image*, 1947.
R. L. Brett, *Fancy and Imagination* (Critical Idiom Series), 1969.
P. N. Furbank, *Reflections on the Word 'Image'*, 1970.

Personification

Ever since Wordsworth wrote his Preface to the 1800 edition of *Lyrical Ballads*, personification has been a rather suspect figure. But Wordsworth himself was careful to qualify his objections to personification.

> Except in a very few instances [he wrote], the Reader will find no personifications of abstract ideas in these volumes, not that I mean to censure such personifications: *they may be well fitted for certain sorts of composition*, but in these Poems I propose to

myself to imitate, and, as far as possible, to adopt the very language of men, and I do not find that such personifications make any regular or natural part of that language.

The phrase in italics is a very important qualification and Wordsworth himself made brilliant use of personification in, for example, his sonnet *On the Extinction of the Venetian Republic*,

> Venice, the eldest child of Liberty.
> She was a maiden City, bright and free;
> No guile seduced, no force could violate;
> And, when she took unto herself a Mate,
> She must espouse the everlasting sea.

Certainly many eighteenth-century poets overworked this figure and one can well understand Wordsworth's reaction to it in the *Lyrical Ballads*. Like other literary currency it becomes thin with constant handling, but it still has a useful life in poetry. Hopkins employs it very simply and directly in stanza fifteen of *The Wreck of the Deutschland*,

> Hope had grown grey hairs,
> Hope had mourning on.

But there is a much more subtle manipulation of it in stanza eleven:

> 'Some find me a sword; some
> The flange and the rail; flame,
> Fang, or flood' goes Death on drum,
> And storms bugle his fame.

Hopkins describes here the variety of ways in which we may meet death. For some it is the death of battle (a sword); for others it is the end of an orderly journey, as when the train arrives at the terminus (the flange and the rail); for others again, accident of some kind (flame, fang, or flood). Perhaps Hopkins had in mind Donne's famous sonnet, 'At the round earth's imagin'd corners', where there is a similar but more extensive list,

> All whom the flood did, and fire shall o'erthrow,
> All whom warre, dearth, age, agues, tyrannies,
> Despair, law, chance, hath slaine. . . .

But Hopkins puts his list into the mouth of a personified Death and the figure suggests a recruiting sergeant with bugle and drum, calling us to the colours. A similar and successful personification of death can be found in Donne's *The Second Anniversary*, where the figure carries the meaning that death is not the end but the beginning of a journey:

> Thinke then, my soule, that death is but a Groome,
> Which brings a Taper to the outward roome,
> Whence thou spiest first a little glimmering light,
> And after brings it nearer to thy sight:
> For such approaches doth heaven make in death.

Symbol

When personification is used on an extended scale it leads naturally to **allegory** in which abstract or general notions are personified in a story which represents some moral or doctrine. The most famous allegory in English is Bunyan's *The Pilgrim's Progress* which converts the Christian doctrine of salvation into the story of Christian's journey from the City of Destruction to the Celestial City, and of how he encounters on the way characters such as Faithful, Hopeful and Despair. Allegory is more than extended personification, however, for some abstractions are represented in non-personified terms. In Bunyan's work Christian, as well as meeting many other characters, has to struggle through the Slough of Despond and is led to visit Vanity Fair. In other allegories, such as *Everyman* and *The Faerie Queene*, we find the same representation of abstract ideas, both in persons and situations.

Symbolism differs from allegory in that allegory often becomes an artificial contrivance, whereby everything on one level of the narrative has a referent (or analogue) on another. Coleridge criticized this tendency to artificiality when he wrote that allegory is 'merely a translation of abstract notions into a picture language, which is itself nothing but an abstraction from objects of the senses'. A symbol, on the other hand, he contended, 'is characterized by a translucence of the special [i.e. the species] in the individual'. Coleridge meant by this that a symbol represents something else, but that when used successfully as a literary figure it is more than an artificial or arbitrary sign. It is not like the circular sign, which informs the motorist that he is approaching the end of a Speed Limit; this is quite arbitrary and could be expressed just as well by some other sign. A symbol is itself a member of the class which it represents. Thus the word *bread* in stanza one of *The Wreck of the Deutschland* is a symbol, for it belongs to a whole class of things (especially food) which sustain life. A symbol is, therefore, no different in kind from *metonym* or *synecdoche*, but the terms *symbol* and *symbolism* are generally employed either when there is a set or cluster of images of a similar kind in a literary work, or when the image is used on an extended scale to represent a complex meaning.

Examples of the first usage can be found in recent Shakespearian criticism. Ever since Caroline Spurgeon's *Motives in the Imagery of Shakespeare's Tragedies* (1930), critics have tended to emphasize Shakespeare's use of symbolism. This has been accompanied by a movement away from attaching importance to the characters in his plays, and a reaction against the kind of criticism to be found in A. C. Bradley's *Shakespearean Tragedy*. It is true that in *Macbeth*, for instance, there is a recurrence of the image of blood (the symbol of guilt and violence), in *Hamlet* of weeds and disease (the symbols of corruption and decay), in *King Lear* of clothes (the symbol of outward appearances and authority). But the recognition of this has had an excessive influence on the interpretation of the plays and has tended to turn them into poems rather than dramatic representations.

Examples of the other usage can be seen in *The Ancient Mariner* and T. S. Eliot's *Four Quartets*. The shooting of the albatross in

The Ancient Mariner is an excellent illustration of what Coleridge himself meant by a symbol. The incident is symbolic of all sin, but is also a particular example of sin, since it illustrates a lack both of respect for life and of humility towards the natural order. In his *Four Quartets* Eliot makes constant use of the symbols of the Fire and the Rose. The one symbolizes God's judgement or wrath, which is not vindictive but purgative, the other symbolizes human achievement, which reaches its supreme height in the perfect man, Jesus Christ.

Symbolism is not, of course, confined to poetry. Dickens's use of the word *fog* at the opening of *Bleak House* is clearly a symbolic one, and at the very beginning of the novel introduces one of the controlling factors in the plot: the confusion, muddle, and delay, in which the Court of Chancery conducts its affairs.

> Fog everywhere. Fog up the river, where it flows among green aits and meadows; fog down the river, where it rolls defiled among the tiers of shipping, and the waterside pollutions of a great (and dirty) city. . . .
> The raw afternoon is rawest, and the dense fog is densest, and the muddy streets are muddiest, near that leaden-headed old obstruction, appropriate ornament for the threshold of a leaden-headed old corporation; Temple Bar. And hard by Temple Bar, in Lincoln's Inn Hall, at the very heart of the fog, sits the Lord High Chancellor in his High Court of Chancery.

Some critics have seen certain symbols, such as water, fire, the rose, the growth of the crops, etc., as what they call archetypal. This term is taken from the psychological writings of Jung, and critics have meant by it that these symbols belong to the 'collective unconscious' of the human race. Such symbols are supposed to have a special emotional power because they evoke racial memories which belong to the unconsciousness of all of us. The danger of this for criticism is that it can lead to reductionism; that is, it can reduce all literary works to the same patterns and obliterate the differences between them. With a critic like

Northrop Frye, however, it is used in a highly sophisticated way to provide what he considers a more scientific criticism. For him criticism should become a 'literary anthropology, concerned with the way that literature is informed by pre-literary categories such as ritual, myth and folk-tale'.

The importance which was given to the symbol after the Romantic Revival led to the development of Symbolism as a movement in modern poetry. Two nineteenth-century French poets in particular, Baudelaire and Mallarmé, made Symbolism an important influence upon modern poetry, and especially upon the earlier work of T. S. Eliot. It is difficult to summarize this movement briefly, but using the terms employed in Chapter One, we can say that Symbolism divorces *poiema* from *logos* and claims that *poiema* is a symbolic structure which carries its own meaning without any relationship to logical discourse. The success of this movement was reinforced by the tendency (derived from depth-psychology) to equate the poetic imagination with the unconscious mind. Even when certain symbols have a private significance for the poet they are often assumed to make an appeal to unexplored depths of the reader's mind. T. S. Eliot expresses something of this in *The Use of Poetry and the Use of Criticism* (1933) when he writes:

> Why, for all of us, out of all that we have heard, seen, felt, in a lifetime, do certain images recur, charged with emotion, rather than others? The song of one bird, the leap of one fish, at a particular place and time, the scent of one flower, an old woman on a German mountain path, six ruffians seen through an open window playing cards at night at a small French railway junction where there was a watermill [cf. Eliot's use of this image in *Journey of the Magi*]: such memories may have symbolic value, but of what we cannot tell, for they come to represent the depths of feeling into which we cannot peer.

The fact that Eliot used such images in his poetry implies that he believed they could have a symbolic significance for his reader. They were supposed to be more than private images, though not necessarily archetypal or mythical. (*v.* below under **Myth.**) As he wrote in *The Sacred Wood*, such images may become part 'of a new object which is no longer personal, because it is a work of art itself'. The work of art uses what is personal, but makes it public by the employment of what Eliot described, in a famous phrase in his essay on *Hamlet* (1919), as an 'objective correlative'. He defined this as 'a set of objects, a situation, a chain of events which shall be the formula of that *particular* emotion' which the poet seeks to communicate.

One consequence of this emphasis upon symbolism is that many twentieth-century poets have felt able largely to dispense with syntax and to write in a language which links image to image rather than statement to statement. In more recent years there has been a reaction to this in the writing of poets whose work observes the rules of syntax. Two of the most distinguished of these are Philip Larkin and Donald Davie.

For Further Reading

G. Wilson Knight, *The Wheel of Fire*, 1930.
Maud Bodkin, *Archetypal Patterns in Poetry*, 1934.
C. S. Lewis, *The Allegory of Love*, 1936.
Frank Kermode, *The Romantic Image*, 1957.
Graham Hough, *Image and Experience*, 1960.
Charles Chadwick, *Symbolism* (Critical Idiom Series), 1972.

Myth

The term *myth* today generally means a story which is known to be untrue, and *mythology* a religious system in which we no longer believe. But the Greek word *muthos* was used by Plato and Aristotle in distinction from *logos*. They meant by it either a traditional story about the gods, or a contrived fable which contained truths beyond the scope of logical demonstration. It was used by Aristotle in the *Poetics* as a synonym for 'plot' or 'fable', but with the understanding that the story was legendary and derived from an earlier period of religious faith. Modern psychology has discerned in such legends truths about human nature that do not depend upon the historicity of the legends. Most Christians today would not object to speaking of the stories of the Creation and Fall as myths in this sense. The word *mythology* can be used even more widely as meaning the framework of belief within which a literary work is created. Thus we can speak of *The Wreck of the Deutschland* as being written with a Christian mythology without impugning the historical truth of the poet's religious beliefs in any way.

Since the end of the seventeenth century and the rise of science, poets have increasingly felt the lack of any mythology to give their work a frame of reference. Man needs a mythology not only to satisfy his emotional needs, but also to order his thinking, and myth is a product of the interplay between *poiema* and *logos* we referred to in Chapter One. At the time of the Romantic Revival poets such as Keats and Shelley tried to revitalize the old classical mythologies, and Wordsworth wrote of the poet's need:

> I'd rather be a pagan suckled in a creed outworn,
> So might I, standing on this pleasant lee,
> Have glimpses that would make me less forlorn;
> Have sight of Proteus rising from the sea,
> Or hear old Triton blow his wreathed horn.

Blake met the need by creating a highly individual mythology from a fusion of his own artistic vision with Swedenborg, Christianity and neo-Platonism. T. S. Eliot referred to this rather unkindly as having been 'put together out of the odds and ends about the house'. More recently, W. B. Yeats constructed a mythology out of his own personal intuition and Irish legend, to give his poetry some kind of framework.

Of all the devices we have been considering in this chapter myth is by far the largest in scale. Indeed, to speak of it as a device at all is inaccurate, for it is not something which operates internally in the work of art, but a framework which gives the work meaning and coherence. Nevertheless, it may have a decisive influence on the other devices we have discussed. Thus the imagery and symbolism of Hopkins's poem are frequently products of the Christian framework in which he writes, and would be meaningless unless the reader appreciated this. In stanza twenty-two, for instance, Hopkins exploits the fact that the number of drowned nuns was five, in order to make a comparison with the sufferings of Christ, who bore five stigmata on his crucified body. The word *stigma* can mean not only a wound but a branding, and he develops this in the image of sheep which are branded by their suffering to show that they belong to Christ. The hand that does the branding is man's not God's, for it was the nuns' compatriots who forced them into exile. Christ himself is often referred to as the lamb of God, for he became the sacrifice which in the Jewish Passover had originally been a lamb. The five nuns are branded as belonging to their master, but the master himself was branded in the same way. And in both instances it was not God, but man who inflicted their suffering.

For Further Reading

Douglas Bush, *Mythology and the Renaissance Tradition in English Poetry*, 1933, and *Mythology and the Romantic Tradition in English Poetry*, 1937.
Philip Wheelwright, 'Poetry, Myth, and Reality', in *The Language of Poetry* (ed. A. Tate), 1942.
Susanne K. Langer, *Philosophy in a New Key*, 1942. *Feeling and Form*, 1953.
E. M. W. Tillyard, *Some Mythical Elements in English Literature*, 1961.

CHAPTER FOUR

Some Further Figures of Meaning
Antithesis, Paradox and Irony

The figures dealt with in the last chapter are all examples of how meaning coalesces in a single image or symbol and of how a multiplicity of meanings can be held together in unity. The name sometimes given to this sort of figure is *trope*. The present chapter is concerned with figures that hold various meanings in balance, contrast or suspension. The basis of this kind of figure is antithesis and not, as in the other, synthesis. The period of English literature which started with Dryden shows a marked increase in antithetical figures and some critics have explained this as the result of the use of the poetic couplet by Augustan poets. The poetic couplet certainly adapts very easily to antithesis, but there is probably a more fundamental reason than this. The development of scientific thought at the end of the seventeenth century made it more difficult to accept the view that images, symbols, metaphors, etc., can express meaning, and the quotation in Chapter One from Sprat's *History of the Royal Society* shows the distrust of tropes that ensued. Augustan poetry moved towards statement as a vehicle of meaning, but still felt the need to express truths which cannot be conveyed in logical discourse and this led to devices in which meaning is balanced between statements.

Antithesis

The rhymed couplet is the poetic form which lends itself most easily to antithesis and the master of this form was Pope. Very often the antithesis is achieved by a skilful use of the caesura (the pause in the line which the sense demands). This is illustrated in the second line of the couplet from the *Essay on Man* where Pope expresses man's equivocal place in the scheme of things,

> Plac'd on this isthmus of a middle state,
> A being darkly wise, and rudely great.

This couplet illustrates not only antithesis but the figure called **oxymoron** which juxtaposes two apparently contradictory terms. 'Darkly wise' and 'rudely great' are both examples of it. The most famous lines which exploit oxymoron are those from Tennyson's *Lancelot and Elaine*,

> His honour rooted in dishonour stood
> And faith unfaithful kept him falsely true.

The last line of stanza twenty-four of *The Wreck of the Deutschland*—'christens her wild-worst Best'—also contains this figure.

The antithetical structure of the couplet was employed by Johnson in *The Vanity of Human Wishes* to express the same sceptical attitude towards man's knowledge and status as in Pope's *Essay on Man*,

> Must helpless man, in ignorance sedate,
> Roll darkling down the torrent of his fate?

Crabbe, though he lived on into the nineteenth century when the couplet was growing unfashionable, was an apt pupil of Pope in this form. The second line of the following quotation shows the same skill in its placing of the caesura to achieve an antithesis,

> She knew that mothers grieved and widows wept,
> And she was sorry, said her prayers and slept.

There are two other figures which depend upon antithesis for their effect. These are **chiasmus** and **zeugma.** Chiasmus is a device by which the order of words in one clause is inverted in a parallel one, as in the line from Pope's *The Temple of Fame*,

> Compos'd his Posture, and his Look Sedate.

Zeugma, which in Greek means 'yoking', refers to the use of a word which stands in the same grammatical relation to two other terms, but with a difference of meaning in each instance. Pope uses it in *The Rape of the Lock* in the couplet,

> Here Thou, Great Anna! whom three Realms obey,
> Dost sometimes Counsel take—and sometimes Tea.

Paradox

At its simplest the paradox is a statement that is apparently self-contradictory, but which contains a truth below the surface. It, too, is based upon antithesis, but when extended and sustained by other figures, gains an importance that demands separate treatment. Donne employed the paradox in this extended manner and some of his poems are built on a series of paradoxes. *The Canonization*, for instance, rests on the paradoxical argument that lovers are saints and deserve canonization of a kind that may be commemorated in secular poetry if not in church-monuments. The following stanza starts with a paradox that depends upon a punning use of the word 'dye' (to consummate love physically):

> Wee can dye by it, if not live by love,
> And if unfit for tombes and hearse
> Our legend be, it will be fit for verse;
> And if no peece of Chronicle we prove,
> We'll build in sonnets pretty rooms;
> As well a well wrought urne becomes
> The greatest ashes, as halfe-acre tombes,
> And by these hymnes, all shall approve
> Us *Canoniz'd* for Love.

Donne could also turn paradox to account in his religious poems and he ends his sonnet on death with the lines:

> One short sleep past, we wake eternally,
> And Death shall be no more, Death thou shalt die.

T. S. Eliot, who is a great admirer of Donne, uses the extended paradox with brilliant effect in *Four Quartets. Little Gidding*, the last poem of the series, opens with a passage which expresses the sense of the soul's awakening that sometimes comes to one in a period of spiritual deadness. It starts with the oxymoron, 'Midwinter spring', and develops the meaning of this image by a series of paradoxes.

> Midwinter spring is its own season
> Sempiternal though sodden towards sundown,
> Suspended in time, between pole and tropic.
> When the short day is brightest, with frost and fire,
> The brief sun flames the ice, on pond and ditches,
> In windless cold that is the heart's heat,
> Reflecting in a watery mirror
> A glare that is blindness in the early afternoon.
> And glow more intense than blaze of branch, or brazier,
> Stirs the dumb spirit: no wind, but pentecostal fire
> In the dark time of the year. Between melting and freezing
> The soul's sap quivers.

Eliot also makes use of paradox in *East Coker*, where again he makes it more effective by combining it with images. Here the passage opens with the paradoxical figure of 'The wounded surgeon', Christ himself.

> The wounded surgeon plies the steel
> That questions the distempered part;
> Beneath the bleeding hands we feel
> The sharp compassion of the healer's art
> Resolving the enigma of the fever chart.
>
> Our only health is the disease
> If we obey the dying nurse
> Whose constant care is not to please
> But to remind of our, and Adam's curse,
> And that, to be restored our sickness must grow worse.

The Wreck of the Deutschland is centred upon the apparent contradiction between God's merciful providence and the heartbreak of human experience, and it, too, expresses religious faith in the language of paradox. The third stanza is one of the passages in the poem where this is most evident. God's will is a thing of terror and yet at the centre of the terror there is a love of which we can be confident because God, in Christ, has experienced the same suffering we are called upon to face. It is in the Mass that the suffering and love of Christ are brought together; at the heart of this liturgical commemoration of God's self-sacrificial love lies the answer to the paradox.

> The frown of his face
> Before me, the hurtle of hell
> Behind, where, where was a, where was a place?
> I whirled out wings that spell
> And fled with a fling of the heart to the heart of the Host.

Irony

Irony at a simple level can exploit antithesis by stating something literally, but with the implication that the opposite is really true. Jane Austen was a gifted exponent of this kind of verbal irony and gives an amusing illustration of it in *Pride and Prejudice* when Mr Bennett addresses his daughter, Mary, who is about to sing again, with the remark, 'That will do extremely well, child. You have delighted us long enough.' In irony there is a reversal of meaning of which we are sometimes immediately aware, but in a gifted writer, sometimes with shock when we recognize his real meaning. In **dramatic irony**, which is often used in tragedy, something may be said or done of which the real significance is appreciated only by the audience. Even more tragic in effect is the kind of dramatic irony occasioned by the hero's good intentions turning to evil results through some quirk of circumstance. (*v.* **Tragedy** in Chapter 2.)

Irony can be extended so that it operates not only internally and locally, but provides a form and framework for the entire work. In the Augustan period the prevailing temper of thought made it difficult to employ a mythological framework seriously and, as we have seen, the mock-epic form became popular The 'mock' use of literary forms (the epic in Pope's *The Rape of the Lock*, the travel story in Swift's *Gulliver's Travels*, Biblical history in Dryden's *Absalom and Achitophel*, etc.) is really an extension of irony, for the form seems to suggest one meaning, but really implies another. The purpose of the whole literary form is reversed. Irony when used on this scale and in this way merges into **satire**, which is the art of making a subject look ridiculous. (See under **Mock-epic** in Chapter 2 and under **Satire** in *Appendix A*.)

The greatest master of irony in English was Swift and a good example of his skill in using it can be seen in the following passage from *A Tale of a Tub*. F. R. Leavis in an essay in *The Common Pursuit* (1952) discusses Swift's irony at some length and especially Swift's sustained deception of the reader until the last moment. This passage is a superb example of 'fooling' the reader until in the final sentence he realizes with a shock that all that has gone before is ironical.

> In the proportion that credulity is a more peaceful possession of the mind than curiosity, so far preferable is that wisdom which converses about the surface to that pretended philosophy which enters into the depth of things, and then comes gravely back with informations and discoveries that in the inside they are good for nothing. The two senses to which all objects first address themselves are the sight and the touch; these never examine farther than the colour, the shape, the size, and whatever other qualities dwell or are drawn by art upon the outward of bodies; and then comes reason officiously with tools for cutting, and opening, and mangling, and piercing, offering to demonstrate that they are not of the same consistence quite through. Now I take all this to be the last degree of perverting nature; one of whose eternal laws it is, to put her best furniture forward. And therefore, in order to save the charges of all such expensive anatomy for the time to come, I do here think fit to inform the reader that in such conclusions as these reason is certainly in the right; and that, in most corporeal beings which have fallen under my cognisance, the out-

side has been infinitely preferable to the in: whereof I have
been farther convinced from some late experiments. Last week
I saw a woman flayed, and you will hardly believe how much
it altered her person for the worse. Yesterday I ordered the
carcase of a beau to be stripped in my presence; when we were
all amazed to find so many unsuspected faults under one suit of
clothes. Then I laid open his brain, his heart, and his spleen: but
I plainly perceived at every operation, that the farther we pro-
ceeded we found the defects increase upon us in number and
bulk: from all which, I justly formed this conclusion to myself,
that whatever philosopher or projector can find out an art to
solder and patch up the flaws and imperfections of nature will
deserve much better of mankind, and teach us a more useful
science, than that so much in present esteem, of widening and
exposing them, like him who held anatomy to be the ultimate
end of physic. And he whose fortunes and dispositions have
placed him in a convenient station to enjoy the fruits of this
noble art; he that can, with Epicurus, content his ideas with the
films and images that fly off upon his senses from the superficies
of things; such a man, truly wise, creams off nature, leaving
the sour and the dregs for philosophy and reason to lap up.
This is the sublime and refined point of felicity, called the
possession of being well deceived; the serene peaceful state of
being a fool among knaves.

For Further Reading

Ian Jack, *Augustan Satire*, 1952.
J. R. Sutherland, *English Satire*, 1958.
Geoffrey Tillotson, *Augustan Studies*, 1961.
A. Pollard, *Satire* (Critical Idiom Series), 1970.
D. C. Muecke, *Irony* (Critical Idiom Series), 1971.

CHAPTER FIVE

Figures of Sound
Rhyme, Alliteration, Assonance and Consonance

A literary work is not only a pattern of meanings but a pattern of sounds. This is particularly true in poetry, which makes a special appeal to the ear. Some critics, especially the Symbolist writers of the late nineteenth century, have argued that poetry is pure sound and not concerned with meaning at all. But it is difficult to maintain this position. The two most radical examples which might be expected to support this argument are (1) nonsense verse, and (2) listening to poetry in a foreign language we do not understand. In both of these our pleasure might be thought to derive solely from the sound. But if we take the opening lines of Lewis Carroll's *Jabberwocky*,

> 'Twas brillig, and the slithy toves
> Did gyre and gimble in the wabe,

we notice that there is more than a pattern of pure sounds. There is a syntactical structure; a sentence form with verbs, subject, and adjectives. Moreover, not all the words are nonsensical; even the word 'slithy', as Humpty Dumpty explained, means 'lithe and slimy'. If we substituted nonsensical sounds for the real words and rewrote the lines as follows,

> Mars brillig, mand ma sithy toves
> Fid gure mand gimble min ma wabe

our pleasure would vanish. Equally, the pleasure of listening to poetry in a language one does not understand is very slight and largely depends upon emphasis or tone. In both instances we try to impose meaning on what we hear.

Pure sound in poetry is an abstraction. Sound reinforces the meaning and is reinforced by the meaning. Even the most onomatopoeic language (*i.e.* language where the sound seems almost identical with the meaning) is considerably less dependent on sound than we might at first think. The American critic, John Crowe Ransom, has shown this in a striking way by taking Tennyson's famous line,

And murmuring of innumerable bees in immemorial elms,

and changing it to

And murdering of innumerable beeves in immemorial elms.

The sound change is negligible, but the quite different meaning has altered the poetic effect drastically. In good poetry meaning and sound fuse together and, as Pope declared in *An Essay on Criticism*, the sound should echo the sense. But Pope recognized that many readers of poetry fail to understand this:

> In the bright muse, though thousand charms conspire,
> Her voice is all these tuneful fools admire;
> Who haunt Parnassus but to please their ear,
> Not mend their minds; as some to church repair,
> Not for the doctrine, but the music there.

Hopkins was an expert in the art of matching the sense and the sound in poetry. Stanza twenty-four of *The Wreck of the Deutschland* provides a good example of his virtuosity. It begins with four lines that are quiet and peaceful, moving easily and employing open vowel sounds. The word *gales* ends this passage with a vigorous sound and leads to a quickening pace, and a staccato movement with the buffeting 'b' sound of *black-about* and *breaker*. The fury rises to a crescendo in the direct speech of 'O Christ, Christ, come quickly', which echoes in the 'c' sound the urgency of the word *calling*. The rhyming of *Wales, gales* and *quails* marks the three stages in the stanza by its emphasis of these key words. *Wales* has a quiet, restful sound which is reinforced by the adjective *pastoral*; *gales* echoes the force of the storm; and *quails* in meaning and sound suggests the overthrow of the storm's victims.

The art of manipulating language in this way is infinitely complex and subtle and is difficult to describe in general terms. But the following are the main devices by which sound is organized to give pattern to a literary work, and especially to poetry.

Rhyme

Rhyme is the matching of the last stressed vowel and all the sounds that follow it, in two or more words. If the rhyme includes an unstressed syllable after the stressed vowel sound it is known as a **feminine rhyme,** but if not, then the rhyme is called **masculine.** Thus in

> John Grubby, who was short and *stout*
> And troubled with religious *doubt*,
> Refused about the age of *three*
> To sit upon the curate's *knee*,

the rhymes are all masculine. But in the following,

> When we two *parted*
> In silence and *tears*,
> Half broken-*hearted*
> To sever for *years*,

parted–hearted is a feminine rhyme and *tears–years* masculine. A feminine rhyme of this kind, where the unstressed syllables are also matched in sound, is called a **double rhyme,** and if there are three rhymed syllables it is called a **triple rhyme.** Triple rhymes are generally used with comic effect, for there is such an unexpected quality about them, and this is increased if the normal word order is altered, or if the pronunciation of the words is forced into yielding a rhyme. Browning uses this device at the end of *The Pied Piper*:

> So, Willy, let me and you *be wipers*
> Of scores out with all men—especial*ly pipers*.

It is possible to have rhymes not only at the end of lines but internally. In stanza twenty-one of *The Wreck of the Deutschland*, the last line,

Storm flakes were scroll-leaved flowers, lily showers—sweet
heaven was astrew in them.

has an internal rhyme, *flowers–showers*, and in stanza six *hushed by* rhymes with *flushed by*.

It is also possible to have **half-rhymes,** in which the rhymed vowels differ and in which even the consonants are not always identically the same. The poet who exploited the half-rhyme and brought it into fashion in modern poetry was Wilfred Owen, who was killed in the first World War. He uses it with fine effect in *Strange Meeting*, of which the following are the opening lines:

It seemed that out of battle I escaped
Down some profound dull tunnel, long since scooped
Through granites which titanic wars had groined.
Yet also there encumbered sleepers groaned,
Too fast in thought or death to be bestirred.
Then, as I probed them, one sprang up, and stared
With piteous recognition in fixed eyes,
Lifting distressful hands as if to bless.

Alliteration

Alliteration is the repetition of matched consonant sounds, generally though not always at the beginning of words. In Old English and medieval poetry it was a characteristic feature, the alliteration being evenly balanced with a regular effect achieved by the caesura (*i.e.* the natural pause that reading demands) in each line. Hopkins deliberately set out to recapture some of the qualities of this older form of English poetry and to use them for his own purpose. If one compares the opening lines of the fourteenth-century poem by Langland, *The Vision of Piers Plowman*, with a stanza from *The Wreck of the Deutschland* the similarities are obvious. *Piers Plowman* begins as follows:

In a somer seson ‖ whan soft was the sonne,
I shope me in shroudes ‖ as I a shepe were,
In habite as an hermite ‖ vnholy of workes,
Went wyde in this world ‖ wondres to here.

Stanza twenty-five of Hopkins reads:

The majesty! ‖ what did she mean?
Breathe, ‖ arch and original Breath.
Is it love in her of the being ‖ as her lover had been?
Breathe, ‖ body of lovely Death.
They were else-minded then, ‖ altogether, the men
Woke thee with a ‖ we are perishing in the weather
                                        of Gennesareth.
Or is it that she cried ‖ for the crown then,
The keener to come at the comfort ‖ for feeling the
                                        combating keen?

There is the same basic pattern in the verse, but the rather monotonous rhythm of Langland has become much more sophisticated in Hopkins and the alliteration much more complex. We
shall deal with his modifications in rhythm in the next chapter,
but we note here his use of double alliteration. In the last line
there are two alliterating sounds, *k* and *f*. Three of the stressed
syllables in the first half-line, and two in the second, alliterate on
k. One unstressed syllable in the first half-line, and one stressed
syllable in the second, alliterate on *f*.

Assonance

Assonance is the repetition of identical or similar vowel sounds
where there is not a full rhyme. It is a favourite device with
Hopkins and occurs throughout *The Wreck of the Deutschland*.
Note how the *i* and *e* sounds form a pattern in stanza six, quite
apart from the full rhymes at the end of the lines:

Not out of his bliss
Springs the stress felt
Nor first from heaven (and few know this)
Swings the stroke dealt—

He likes to use it, together with alliteration, in compound words and phrases such as, *dappled*-with-*damson*; *lush-kept, plush-capped*; *martyr-master*; and often combines it with the half-rhyme.

Consonance

Consonance is the repetition of identical or similar consonants with a change in the intervening vowel sounds. Hopkins uses it frequently, and again often in compounds such as: *heaven–haven*; *stars . . . storms*; *Father* and *fondler*; *Father . . . feathers*; etc.

Hopkins's effects generally depend not upon an exact consonance, but upon a highly intricate mingling of all the sound devices we have described. Stanza thirteen of his poem, for instance, makes one realize not only this but also his skill in placing words in the right places. One is reminded of Coleridge's definition of poetry as 'the best words in the best order'. The stanza opens in language that is almost matter-of-fact, but the placing of *sweeps* and *Hurling*, as well as their sound and meaning, makes us feel the force of the wind. By putting *the haven* as the object of the verb *Hurling* he makes us conscious of the speed of the ship. The stanza slows down with the phrase 'so the sky keeps' and with the emphasis on *keeps*. But this is merely to reinforce our sense of the continuous implacability of the elements, and the stanza gathers speed again with 'And the sea flint-flake'. The reversal of the usual word order in the line,

> Sitting Eastnortheast, in cursed quarter, the wind;

stresses *wind*, and placing *deeps* at the very end of the stanza gives the word added meaning and menace. Poetry is not merely a matter of the sounds and meanings of words but of their order, and this leads us to the next chapter.

CHAPTER SIX

The Elements of Prosody

Prosody is a big subject and we cannot deal with all its complexities in one short chapter. It embraces all aspects of versification including metre, stanza forms and the subjects dealt with in the last chapter. We shall be concerned here primarily with metre, and for details of the main stanza forms the reader should consult the *Select Glossary of Literary Terms* in *Appendix A*. One of the difficulties in discussing metre is that there is no agreed terminology, but the following are the main elements in the organization of sounds in metrical patterns.

Accent or Stress

In ordinary English speech certain syllables or words are stressed or accentuated, either because of phonetic convention, or because of the demands of meaning.

Phonetic convention varies from age to age, and from country to country, even where the same language is spoken. This can be illustrated by the pronunciation of the word *miscellany*. In the eighteenth century it was pronounced *miscellány*; in the nineteenth century, *miscéllany*; and there is a tendency today to pronounce it *míscellany*. This is an example of how we have tended in England to shift the stress or accent towards the first syllable of a word. In America, on the other hand, the stress or accent has remained where it was in the eighteenth century and the pronunciation is still *miscellány*.

We also stress words in spoken English to indicate meaning. In the following sentence,

I want to buy a new red car,

we can change the meaning according to the word we stress. '*I* want to buy a new red car' suggests that the person I am addressing is thinking of buying something else. 'I *want* to buy a new red car' suggests some doubt in the listener's mind about my intentions. 'I want to *buy* a new red car' rules out borrowing or hiring. And so we can go on, shifting the stress from word to word to change the meaning.

Certain writers have contended that metre is no more than the stressing of ordinary speech tidied up and arranged in patterns of sound. But while it is true that poetry cannot ignore the rhythms of ordinary speech (i.e. the kinds of stress we have referred to above) some sorts of poetry depend for their effect on the super-imposing of a further pattern of sound upon ordinary speech. In any case, if the stressing of certain syllables is in a fairly regular pattern of sound, so that the ear is led to expect a stress in the place where the rest of the pattern suggests it, then a poetic metre is achieved.

Such patterns can be simple and obvious, with a good thumping rhythm. Kipling's *Barrack-Room Ballads* depend a good deal on this kind of rhythm, as in,

> Duke's son, cook's son, son of a belted earl,
> Colonel's lady, Judy O'Grady;

and an excellent illustration is found in Vachel Lindsay's *General William Booth enters into Heaven*, where the metre follows the beat of a Salvation Army band,

> Booth led boldly with his big bass drum,
> (Are you washed in the blood of the Lamb?)
> . . . .
> Oh, shout Salvation! It was good to see
> Kings and Princes by the Lamb set free.
> The banjos rattled and the tambourines
> Jing-jing-jingled in the hands of Queens.

Emphatic rhythms of this kind can often echo or suggest the effect of physical action. A well-known example is Browning's *How They Brought the Good News from Ghent to Aix*, which reproduces the rhythm of a galloping horse,

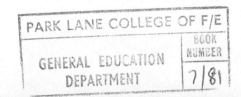

> I sprang to the stirrup, and Joris, and he;
> I galloped, Dirck galloped, we galloped all three.

But not all rhythms are as strong as these, and in lyric poetry the metre may be a very subtle and delicate one.

Quantity

By *quantity* is meant the length of the vowel sound in a syllable. The vowel *a* may be pronounced as long or short and we mark it *ā* for long (as in *raft*) and *ǎ* for short (as in *map*). Latin verse is based upon quantity and organizes its sound effects into patterns of long and short vowel sounds divided into feet. A foot in Latin verse is composed of two or three vowel sounds and the four commonest feet used by Latin poets to create metrical patterns are

The **Trochee:**   long-short (/ ⌣)
               (This can be remembered by Coleridge's 'Trochee trips from long to short'.)
The **Iambus:**   short-long (⌣ /)
The **Dactyl:**   long-short-short (/ ⌣ ⌣)
               (This can be remembered from the fact that *dactyl* is the Greek word for *a finger*, which has one long joint and two short ones.)

The **Anapaest:** short-short-long (⌣ ⌣ /)

There are two other feet, which do not form any metres in themselves, but are used to vary the pattern and avoid monotony. These are

The **Spondee:** long-long (/ /)
The **Pyrrhic:** short-short (⌣ ⌣)

It is very common to scan English verse by dividing it into these feet and by counting a stressed syllable as a long vowel and an unstressed as a short. Most of our poets from the Renaissance onwards have been familiar with Latin poetry and many of them up to the nineteenth century spent some of their school-days in composing Latin verse. A great deal of seventeenth and eighteenth-century poetry comes very close to Latin in its metrical forms. Examples of classical metres are easy to find in English poetry.

Iambic Metre

The iambic metre comes closest to natural English speech and when unrhymed and arranged in five-feet lines is called **blank-verse.** Shakespeare's plays are mostly in blank-verse, as are *Paradise Lost*, Wordsworth's *The Prelude*, and many other poems. The following lines from *Gorboduc* provide an illustration of regular blank-verse, but we rarely meet it in such a regular form, since this would lead to monotony.

> And is | it thus? | And doth | he so | prepare
> Against | his broth|er as | his mort|al foe?
> And now | while yet | his ag|ed fath|er lives?

But iambic metre can also be used, with rhyme, and in lines of varying length, as in Wordsworth's Ode, *Intimations of Immortality*,

> There was | a time | when mead|ow, grove, | and stream,
> The earth, | and ev|ery com|mon sight,
> To me | did seem
> Appa|relled in | celest|ial light,
> The glor|y and | the fresh|ness of | a dream.

Trochaic Metre

The trochaic metre is quite frequent in English poetry, though not so common as iambic. The following example is taken from Longfellow's *A Psalm of Life*,

Tell me | not, in | mournful | numbers,
Life is | but an | empty | dream!
For the | soul is | dead that | slumbers,
And things | are not | what they | seem,

but here the second and fourth lines are slightly irregular in having a final stressed monosyllable instead of a trochee.

Dactylic Metre

Browning's *The Lost Leader* provides a good illustration of dactylic metre:

Just for a | handful of | silver he | left us,
Just for a | riband to | stick in his | coat—
Found the one | gift of which | fortune be|reft us,
Lost all the | others she | lets us de|vote

Again it will be noticed that the second and fourth lines are slightly irregular and that the final feet are not dactyls. It is unusual to find verse written in complete and regular dactylic or anapaestic metre.

Anapaestic Metre

An example of anapaestic metre can be seen in Byron's poem

The Assyr|ian came down | like a wolf | on the fold,
And his co|horts were gleam|ing in pur|ple and gold.

From these examples we can see that the feet may be in lines of different length. The technical names for such lines are as follows: a line of one foot is a **monometer,** one of two feet a **dimeter,** of three feet a **trimeter,** of four feet a **tetrameter,** of five feet a **pentameter,** of six feet a **hexameter,** of seven feet a **heptameter,** of eight feet an **octameter.** Thus blank-verse can be called unrhymed iambic pentameters. In addition, verse can be organized in stanza patterns such as the **couplet** (two rhyming lines), the **tercet** (a three-line stanza, generally with a single rhyme), the **quatrain** (a four-line stanza with one or two rhymes). The couplet and quatrain are the commonest forms but there are longer and more complicated stanza forms. See the *Select Glossary of Literary Terms* in *Appendix A*, for **couplet, terza rima, rhyme royal, ottava rima,** the **Spenserian stanza,** and **sonnet.**

Nearly all English poetry is written with departures from the metrical pattern. Complete regularity of metre would be monotonous and most poets introduce irregular feet. These can be inverted feet, unstressed or stressed syllables where the ear expects the reverse, or the stressing of a syllable for emphasis of meaning where the metrical pattern does not demand it.

Some poets have contended that English verse can be written according to the rules that govern the use of quantity in Latin verse. Spenser and Gabriel Harvey in the Elizabethan period, and Robert Bridges at the beginning of this century, composed verse that employed quantity rather than stress, but these attempts are really *tours de force* and rest upon the manipulation of long and short vowel sounds that correspond to stressed and unstressed syllables. Although Latin verse has obviously had a great effect upon English, stress or accent is a far more important factor than quantity.

Very often a regular pattern of stressed syllables is counterpointed by feet which are irregular because they use the stressing of ordinary speech to achieve emphasis of meaning. In the *Epilogue to the Satires*, Pope, for instance, has the following couplet,

'Ye Rev'rend Atheists!'—'Scandal! name them, Who?'—
'Why that's the thing you bid me not to do,'

in which the irregularity of the first line emphasizes the meaning and also provides a counterpoint for the regular second line.

Some poetry tends to scan regularly, but there is also poetry in which the stresses of ordinary speech and the stresses of a metrical pattern combine to provide a more intricate rhythm. Jonson condemned Donne for 'not keeping accent', but Coleridge recognized that 'if you take breath' and read Donne as the sense requires, his poetry has a pleasing rhythmical pattern. One can say that poetry ranges between two extremes; at one end of the scale the sense reveals the rhythm and at the other end the rhythm throws the meaning into relief.

In his preface to *Christabel*, Coleridge laid down what he thought was a new principle in scansion.

> The metre of the *Christabel* [he wrote] is not, properly speaking, irregular, though it may seem so from its being founded on a new principle, namely, that of counting, in each line, the accents, not the syllables. Though the latter may vary from seven to twelve, yet in each line the accents will be found to be only four. Nevertheless this occasional variation in number of syllables is not introduced wantonly, or for the mere ends of convenience, but in correspondence with some transition in the nature of the imagery or passion.

What Coleridge is saying here is that stress is the foundation of his metre in *Christabel*, and that irregularities in the number of syllables arise because he is using language most appropriate for the expression of his thought or feeling ('imagery or passion'). This was new when compared with most eighteenth and late seventeenth century poetry, but it was not entirely new, for medieval and some later poetry was based on this practice. Hopkins took the principle even further and invented a metrical system called **sprung-rhythm,** which he explains at some length in the Preface to his *Poems*. Sprung-rhythm recognizes that stress and not quantity is the governing factor in native English poetry and he based his practice on a more sophisticated version of what he discovered in Old and Middle English poetry and in the ballad.

Hopkins proposed that the stressed syllable should be regarded

as the first syllable in each foot and that every time a stress oc-
curred it should mark the beginning of a new foot. This would
produce four kinds of foot: a stressed monosyllable, a trochee, a
dactyl, and what he called a *First Paeon*—a stressed syllable
followed by three unstressed. Sprung-rhythm is close to the
rhythm of ordinary speech and uses stress to achieve a metrical
structure in which form and meaning reinforce each other with
remarkable effect. But Hopkins uses alliteration, compound
words, run-on lines (*i.e.* lines where the meaning carries the
reader over to the next line with little or no pause), as well as all
the other devices of sound described in the last chapter, and these
give his verse an intricacy that makes it much more highly
charged than ordinary speech. The second stanza of *The Wreck
of the Deutschland* scans as follows and shows the placing of stress
and the great number of unstressed syllables.

I did say | yes
O at | lightning and | lashed | rod;
Thou heardst me | truer than | tongue con|fess
Thy | terror, O | Christ, O | God;
Thou knowest the | walls, | altar and | hour and | night:
The | swoon of a | heart that the | sweep and the | hurl of
thee | trod
Hard | down with a | horror of | height:
And the | midriff a | strain with | leaning of, | laced with
| fire of | stress.

When we add to all these devices of sound and rhythm Hopkins's
vocabulary, with its words of Anglo-Saxon derivation, and his
concentrated syntax, we realize something of the great artistry of
his poetry.

For Further Reading

T. S. Osmond, *English Metrists*, 1921.

P. F. Baum, *The Principles of English Versification*, 1922.

L. Abercrombie, *Principles of English Prosody*, 1923.

Karl Shapiro, *English Prosody and Modern Poetry*, 1947.

J. Thompson, *The Founding of English Metre*, 1961

Robert Bridges (ed.), *Poems of Gerard Manley Hopkins*, 1918, Author's Preface.

John Pick (ed.), *A Hopkins Reader*, 1953.

G. S. Fraser, *Metre, Rhyme and Free Verse* (Critical Idiom Series), 1970.

CHAPTER SEVEN

Some Hints on Style

The following is not meant to be any more than what the title of the chapter indicates. It would be impossible to give here any detailed advice on English composition and usage. For this the reader is recommended to consult the books listed at the end of the chapter.

Besides being a medium of communication, language is a means of thinking. Unless we train ourselves to use language correctly we cannot think clearly and still less can we communicate our thoughts to others. Logic is the most rigorous attempt to express thought in words and the logician tries to make his words as exact and unambiguous as he can. But logic is limited in its range and is concerned only with the intellectual content of words. Nevertheless, in using language of any kind we should first try to learn to use it exactly. This will mean not only having a clear idea of a word's denotation (*i.e.* the object it specifically refers to), but also its connotation (*i.e.* the association of meanings that cluster around it). A writer should use a good dictionary and should train himself to be aware of the shades of meaning and association that a word carries. This training is most effectively acquired by reading, and one of the best ways of achieving a good style is to read good literature. But writing is also a craft and like other crafts improves with practice. If you wish to write well you must write assiduously. Reading and writing provide a better preparation than the formal study of grammar and composition, though this does not mean that the latter is useless.

There are no hard and fast rules for using words, for language is not fixed and dead but always growing. There are certain conventions which we should do well to observe, because they are the accepted conventions of the day, but even these change with the times. Many would still regard it as bad usage to employ the word *like* (adjective) in place of *as* (conjunction), *e.g.* in the following sentence, 'I think we need to keep our railway lines open. Our roads are overcrowded *like* [as] the Dutch ones are.' But the practice is now widespread and may become standard English. On the other hand to write, 'The plans for a new railway system are centred round the need to move goods more quickly,' is bad writing, for something can only be centred *on* and not centred *round*. In the second case change should be resisted, because it reflects sloppy thinking. We may smile at the card in the small outfitter's window, which reads: 'Pair of black man's trousers—£3.' But consider the following from a report of a conference on the *Problem of Adolescence*: 'This thorny question exercised most groups and reflected the quicksands of our changing social pattern which engulfs young and old alike.' Can a question (thorny or otherwise) reflect 'the quicksands'? And what engulfs young and old alike? It can hardly be the 'social pattern', but if it is 'the quicksands', the verb should be 'engulf'. The metaphors implied or expressed by 'thorny', 'reflected' and 'quicksands' are not just mixed but hopelessly muddled.

In the following, 'Having told the Headmaster I was going on holiday next day, my school report was ready in the morning,' it sounds as if my school report told the Headmaster. This is an example of what is called 'the dangling participle', but clear thinking as much as grammar would have prevented the mistake. Sometimes, however, a knowledge of grammar is important. In the following sentence, 'Children having bicycles often causes parents anxiety,' the word 'having' is not a participle, but a verbal noun and demands the word 'children's' in front of it. The subject of the sentence cannot be 'children' since the verb 'causes' is singular. If we feel that 'children's' sounds pedantic then at least we should make the verb plural.

There is no one style appropriate to all occasions, of course, and different subjects require different forms of expression. But in his little *Tractate on Education*, Milton gave some valuable advice when he wrote that the language of poetry is 'simple, sensuous and passionate'. We shall not go far wrong even in writing prose if we keep these qualities in mind.

Simplicity need not mean dullness, provided it is accompanied by the two other qualities, whereas over-ornateness is a constant temptation to the writer. There are occasions when a highly stylized form is appropriate. In writing to officers of the Fleet, officials at the Admiralty until recently began their letters with, 'I am commanded by My Lords Commissioners of the Admiralty to acquaint you that . . .', and in reply, the officers of the Fleet used the phrase, 'Be pleased to inform Their Lordships . . .' This was a pleasing convention which it was a pity to drop. It gave a certain dignity to the occasion and made the writer conscious of a tradition. But for the writing most of us have to do it is dangerous to mount the high-horse. Worst of all is to mix styles. In the report of the conference quoted above, the writer refers to the address of a schoolmaster in these terms:

> He avoided happily the pitfall of pedagogic exhortation and in a quiet commonsense manner, painted the picture of young people open to guidance of the right sort by the right people. Here, of course, was the 64,000 dollar question.

The phrase 'He avoided happily the pitfall of pedagogic exhortation' is a brash example of ornate language and means simply 'He did not give them schoolmasterly advice.' But to end with the cliché, 'the 64,000 dollar question', introduces bathos. And does one generally paint noisily? And is the word 'open' the right one? It is best to avoid phrases such as 'having regard to' (instead of 'since'), 'this day and age' (instead of 'now'), and 'ways and means' (instead of simply 'ways'). They are not only stilted but hackneyed.

By 'sensuous' Milton meant what we would describe as sensory or concrete. It is best to use abstractions sparingly and, if we use them, at any rate to get their meanings correct. In the report already quoted, the following passage occurs:

> They did get, however, a refreshing aeration of the difficulties faced by young folk, some sensible suggestions of ways and means of ameliorating them and perhaps above all, an opportunity for personally facing up to the questions posed.

The word 'aeration' can mean 'airing', but is generally used nowadays for the chemical operation of exposing a substance to oxygen. 'Ameliorating' means 'improving', but you do not 'improve' difficulties, you 'overcome' them. And the last phrase could be better expressed by 'an opportunity of facing these questions'.

The social sciences have popularized a jargon which depends heavily on vague abstractions. The following is from the prospectus of a 'progressive' school:

> Essential to our beliefs is the conviction that the inner motivation and drive of the pupil are the basic elements in effective personal achievement and learning. Our programme, system, and teaching are designed to guide the pupil and help him utilize his resources efficiently and effectively.

Why 'inner motivation'? Can one have 'outer motivation', and does 'motivation' mean any more than 'drive'? And does 'basic' add anything to the word 'elements'? The whole passage could be written much more simply:

> We believe that the important thing in education is the motivation of the pupil himself and our teaching is designed to help him make the fullest use of his own resources.

Not all jargon is bad. There may be a technical jargon which makes communication easier. This is true of law and medicine and of other specialized professions. But the jargon of many business letters often seems inexcusable. The habit of indicating the date by *ult.* and *prox.* and addressing the reader as 'your goodself' is distasteful. Language is so much the reflection of the writer's personality that one suspects the ability, the efficiency and even the integrity of a writer who cannot express himself clearly without needless jargon.

Slang is not the same as jargon. It is often an important means by which language grows and is a sign of virility. The slang of today may become the accepted usage of tomorrow. The word *posh*, for instance, started as slang. According to one account, it was used to mark the luggage of privileged passengers bound for the Far East who had cabins on the cool side of the ship, and signified, 'Port Outward, Starboard Home'. A new word or phrase, such as 'Angry Young Man', or an old word used in a new way, such as 'square', can be an attempt to chart a new experience. But nothing is worse than out-of-date slang that has not been assimilated into the language. The Angry Young Man was certainly a feature of society and literature in the 1950s and it was useful to have a phrase that hit him off so well. But the term had a limited life. To use such a phrase now is to fail to recognize that language is constantly growing. Slang that has outlived its usefulness is akin to the cliché. The writer who uses clichés betrays the fact that he cannot think for himself. The person who first used the metaphor of the brake and accelerator, to describe the Government's policy of alternately curbing and stimulating the country's economy, was using language vividly. But the figure is now as hackneyed as 'the ship of state' or 'the wind of change'.

The third adjective Milton applied to poetry was 'passionate', by which he meant 'with feeling'. Feeling implies sincerity and conviction. Simple and concrete language, when it avoids clichés and expresses original thought in a fresh and vivid way, will convey better than anything else the qualities of sincerity and conviction.

In the preceding chapters we have looked at some of the devices used by the literary artist. A too self-conscious use of these devices might lead to an artificial style, and the beginner should use them with care. 'Look after the sense and the sounds will look after themselves,' may not be entirely true, but it contains some good advice. If we learn to express ourselves clearly, simply and sincerely, we shall find that this discipline will have taught us the discretion needed before we move on to more elaborate forms of writing.

For Further Reading

H. W. Fowler, *A Dictionary of Modern English Usage*, 1926.
H. J. C. Grierson, *Rhetoric and English Composition*, 1945.
Bonamy Dobrée, *Modern Prose Style*, 1934.
Ernest Gowers, *Plain Words*, 1948.
R. Quirk, *The Use of English*, 1962.
William Strunk, Jr. and E. B.White, *The Elements of Style*, 1962.

CHAPTER EIGHT

A Note on Literary Criticism

No great critics have thought that literary criticism was the application of general principles to particular works. Contrary to what is often thought, Aristotle was not laying down general rules, but analysing the practice of the great tragic dramatists of ancient Greece. At certain periods attempts were made to codify his observations into a set of universal principles, but this was never done by the good critic.

In general, criticism has swung between two poles of explanation. At one extreme is the kind of criticism that emphasizes the feelings, taste and reactions of the reader or (in dramatic forms) the audience; at the other is the kind that concentrates on some quality in the work itself. These are rarely divided sharply and most theories of criticism and most critical judgements combine both of these.

Theories and judgements that refer to some quality in the work of literature itself also fall into two classes. In one this quality is explained in formal terms, *e.g.* the way in which the work conforms to some ideal of the *genre* in which it is written, its language, its metrical excellence, the pattern it creates, or even some indefinable quality called beauty or excellence. In the other, literary value is explained in terms outside the work: whether it reflects our own experience, whether it gives pleasure, whether it is morally improving, whether it is psychologically therapeutic, or whether it will be politically useful. Many critical theories and judgements, again, manage to combine several of these.

The philosopher Wittgenstein said that reasons in aesthetics are of the nature of further descriptions. By this he meant that critical judgements are really talk *about* the work in question and

the ways it affects us, and that all we can do to justify our judgements is to engage in this kind of talk and ask others to look at
the work in the light of our description of it. There are no rules
or principles, he maintained, which govern this kind of discussion.
Nevertheless, we can discern in the history of literary criticism
different kinds of 'languages' or systems of thought, in which
critics have carried on the discussion, and certain 'models' or
analogies by reference to which they have described literary
works.

Two of the key concepts, for instance, in Aristotle's theory of
tragedy are *mimesis* (representation) and *katharsis* (purgation).
We have referred already to the fact that Aristotle chose these
terms in order to answer the charges made against literature by
Plato. *Katharsis* is an analogy based upon medical practice and
suggests that tragedy by purging our emotions has a healing
effect upon the mind. Aristotle never suggested this as the purpose
of tragedy—it was simply a by-product—but it has led to a long
line of psychological theories of literary value. In our own day
I. A. Richards has described literary value in terms of a balance
of what he called 'appetencies' and has suggested that good
literature is therapeutic. Edmund Wilson (*The Wound and the
Bow*, 1941) described art as the product of neurosis, and saw the
writer as one who tries to heal himself by symbolizing his conflict in his work.

Aristotle's concept of *mimesis* has had an even greater influence.
In the Elizabethan period it was married to Christian doctrine
and led to the view that Nature, although a work of art, is a
fallen and imperfect world, whereas the poet represents a vision
of the world as it should be or as it was before the Fall. As Sidney
put it in his *Apologie for Poetrie*, the world of Nature 'is brasen,
the Poets only deliver a golden'. By interpreting *mimesis* as
merely 'copying', later generations explained the poetic imagination as simply a mirror, and for some time criticism was
bedevilled by a doctrine of verisimilitude which proved very
restrictive.

The Romantic period, in reaction to this, evolved a theory of the imagination as creative. The description of the poet as a creator, which we find in the work of Coleridge (a key figure in the growth of Romanticism), is clearly the product of analogical thinking. In his letters Coleridge refers to the poetic imagination as 'a divine analogue', and in the famous Chapter XIII of his *Biographia Literaria*, where he defines the poetic imagination, he calls it 'a repetition in the finite mind of the eternal act of creation in the infinite I AM'. Coleridge was a Christian, but in the hands of some other Romantic poets and critics, his doctrine became the theory that the artist is God himself. We see this portrayed in Shelley's *Prometheus Unbound*, where the figure of Prometheus chained in torment on the rock for his rebellion against the gods, is not only that of the political rebel but of the artist who seeks to overthrow the old order and establish a new heaven as well as a new earth.

The Victorian period was the age not of the rebel but of the 'honest doubter', who believed in 'good' rather than God. The figures who best represent this *zeitgeist* are Matthew Arnold and George Eliot. Their influence is still strong in literary criticism and has led to the view that literary value can be defined in terms of moral sensibility. Linked with this is the new interest in sociology and the tendency to see literature as having a duty to improve society and the individual. This is not entirely new, for the Renaissance critic also believed that literature should instruct as well as delight. What is perhaps novel is the insistence that we judge a work good or bad according to whether it reflects the forces that form contemporary society. These forces are often a matter of opinion rather than fact, and the result must sometimes be a partisan kind of criticism. We see this in an extreme form in Marxist criticism which, in the name of 'social realism', judges a work according to whether it displays conflict in terms of dialectical materialism and the class struggle.

The question that emerges from the above is whether one 'model' or one conceptual framework is better than another for criticism. Even if we agree with Wittgenstein, we might still believe that some 'models' and some systems of thought are better than others for helping the critic to make descriptive statements about literature. But the harsh fact is that today there is no generally accepted 'model' or conceptual system, whether religious, metaphysical or even moral, within which critics can, work in agreement.

Perhaps the kind of criticism most popular today is that based on close textual analysis. One must be grateful for the emphasis given in the literary criticism of the last few decades to the close analysis of literary texts, but two reservations need to be made. The first is that the methods used often favour an understanding of short passages rather than an appreciation of the work as a whole and of literary *genres* as such. The other is that this approach tends to ascribe greater value to the work which is complex rather than simple, and to elevate ambiguity, symbolism, irony, multiplicity of meaning, etc., above plain narrative or simple lyricism.

A further question arises in what we call 'practical criticism'. Is the poem (or other work) autonomous and self-explanatory, or is the critic free to go outside the poem in order to 'explain' it? In many instances 'the poem on the table' is clearly not entirely self-explanatory and we need all the help we can get from study-ing the context in which it was written. A good example of this is the following poem by Thomas Hardy.

'The Shadow on the Stone'

I went by the Druid stone
That broods in the garden white and lone,
And I stopped and looked at the shifting shadows
That at some moments fall thereon
From the tree hard by with a rhythmic swing,
And they shaped in my imagining
To the shade that a well-known head and shoulders
Threw there when she was gardening.

I thought her behind my back,
Yea, her I long had learned to lack,
And I said: 'I am sure you are standing behind me,
Though how do you get into this old track?'
And there was no sound but the fall of a leaf
As a sad response; and to keep down grief
I would not turn my head to discover
That there was nothing in my belief.

Yet I wanted to look and see
That nobody stood at the back of me;
But I thought once more: 'Nay, I'll not unvision
A shape which, somehow, there may be'.
So I went on softly from the glade,
And left her behind me throwing her shade,
As she were indeed an apparition—
My head unturned lest my dream should fade.

This poem is discussed at some length by C. B. Cox and A. E. Dyson in *The Practical Criticism of Poetry*, in which they rightly direct our attention to the origins of the poem in the grief and guilt felt by Hardy after the death of his wife, Emma. Without this information the reader would lose a great deal of the ambiguities of thought and feeling which run through the poem and which disturbed Hardy's memories of his wife. It is not only the ambiguity of certain words (e.g. *shade* can mean *shadow* or *spirit*) but the painful and honest attempt by Hardy to explore and express his own ambivalence which informs our reading. The echoes of the story of Orpheus and Eurydice which are heard in the last stanza have a greater impact when we realise that Orpheus was a poet as Hardy was. Similarly the irony of the poem is deepened when related to our knowledge of the conflict between head and heart in Hardy's attitude to religious belief.

Contextual information of this kind can be invaluable but is not a substitute for a sensitive reading of the text itself. Even the discriminating discussion in the book referred to overlooks, for instance, the significance of the poem's title. If the tree is an image of Hardy's wife then surely the stone is an emblem of the poet himself who 'broods in the garden white and lone', and, if this is so, the word *Druid* takes on overtones of meaning associated with the magic powers of poetry. This kind of significance may be prompted by information that lies outside the text, but depends upon an awareness developed only by close reading and reflection.

The awareness is concerned with language, of course, with the meanings and nuances of words, with the language patterns, with style. The discipline of linguistics is also concerned with language and in recent years attempts have been made to bring literature and linguistics together in the study of literary stylistics. Any endeavour to describe more precisely the use of language in literature is to be welcomed and stylistics does provide a vocabulary which enables us to identify and discuss linguistic features of a literary work. But it has certain limitations. Of the three questions implicit in practical criticism, What is the poem saying? How does it say it? How successfully does it achieve a synthesis of the two to produce a work of art?, stylistics is concerned only with the second and even here can say little about such features as symbol and myth. In reading Hardy's poem it would not detect, for instance, the echoes of the Orpheus and Eurydice story. It is not concerned with the third question for it addresses itself only to fact and not to value. In the guise of semantics it may attempt an answer to the first of these questions but cannot in its own right give attention to the kind of contextual information referred to above which often governs the meaning of a poem. It treats the poem as a self-contained verbal object, whereas a poem is more than this. A poem is rather a seeming object which mediates not only between the poet and the reader, but between the reader and his experience; unlike other forms of discourse it both makes something and says something. It engages what Coleridge called 'the whole soul of man'; his intellect, his emotions, and his moral, spiritual, and aesthetic sensibility.

In practice many critics who make less than totalitarian claims for stylistics would counter the objections raised above and would regard a two-way traffic in and out of the poem in terms of language as desirable. They would claim that the linguistic structure of a poem has a reciprocal relationship with the world outside the poem, and that the language of the poet himself is organically related to the resources of language, both past and present, available in dictionaries, grammars, rhetorical figures, and conventional usages. French structuralism demonstrates in a critic like Roland Barthes the possibilities laid open by bringing together the internal analysis of a particular text and the external analysis of its cultural *milieu*. Barthes himself brings to this task Marxism, existentialism, and psychoanalysis, and Lévi-Strauss anthropology and mythology, in support of structural linguistics. In their insistence that literature is a product of the cultural and social order in which it occurs and dependent upon the structures to which that order gives rise, one may discern perhaps a return to tradition rather than a departure from it.

All great poetry, in T. S. Eliot's fine phrase, is 'a raid upon the inarticulate' and there are many languages of criticism which attempt to describe this venture. The task is made immeasurably difficult because the poet is often operating at the extreme boundaries of communication, defying all the rules in his attempt to bring experience under the domination of words. It is unlikely that any one of these languages will have a monopoly of accuracy in its report of this process, but one which consists of ready-made rules is likely to be least successful.

For Further Reading

A. Warren and R. Wellek, *Theory of Literature*, 1949.
R. S. Crane, *The Languages of Criticism and the Structure of Poetry*, 1953.
M. H. Abrams, *The Mirror and the Lamp*, 1953.
G. Watson, *The Literary Critics*, 1962.
W. Righter, *Logic and Criticism*, 1963.
C. B. Cox and A. E. Dyson, *The Practical Criticism of Poetry*, 1965.
G. C. Hough, *An Essay on Criticism*, 1966.
Malcolm Bradbury and David Palmer (ed.), *Contemporary Criticism*, 1970.
Raymond Chapman, *Linguistics and Literature: An Introduction to Stylistics*, 1973.

A Select Glossary of Literary Terms not included
in the text [1]

Alexandrine. A line of verse composed of six iambic feet. It is a long and slow line. *Cf.* Pope's

> A needless Alexandrine ends the song,
> That, like a wounded snake, drags its slow length along,

where the second line is itself an alexandrine. (*v.* **Spenserian Stanza.**)

Antistrophe. In the Greek drama the chorus sometimes chanted a *strophe* as they moved to the left, an *antistrophe* as they moved to the right, and an *epode* as they stood still. (*v.* **Ode.**) The word is sometimes used in rhetoric to mean a repetition of words in reverse order.

Apostrophe. A rhetorical figure in which a speaker or writer interrupts his discourse to address a person or thing directly.

Ballad. The ballad is a song that tells a story. Generally the term refers to the medieval *folk-ballad* which was handed down by oral tradition. A common stanza form for this was the rhyming quatrain in alternate four-stress and three-stress lines, *e.g. Sir Patrick Spens*, which begins,

> The king sits in Dumferline towne,
> Drinking the blude-red wine:
> 'O whar will I get a skeely skipper
> To sail this ship of mine?'

The ballad continued into modern times with the *street-ballad* which often celebrated some item of public news. The ballad has often been adopted by later poets as a literary form, e.g. *Lyrical Ballads* of Wordsworth and Coleridge, and Wilde's *Ballad of Reading Gaol*. (*v.* M. Hodgart, *The Ballads*, 1950.)

Chorus. In Greek drama the chorus was a band of singers and dancers. In the great period of Greek tragedy the chorus often provided a moral or religious commentary on the play. Milton uses a chorus in *Samson Agonistes* in this way, but in Shakespeare, and Elizabethan drama generally, the chorus is one person who speaks the prologue and

---

[1] Two books which will be found useful are M. H. Abrams, *A Glossary of Literary Terms* (much fuller than that given here) and F. W. Bateson, *A Guide to English Literature* (which provides full bibliographies and commentaries on what to read).

epilogue. Some critics have seen characters like the Fool in *King Lear* as taking over the function of the Greek tragic chorus.

The term is also used to refer to the refrain of a song in which all the company join in the singing.

Couplet. The couplet is a pair of metrical rhyming lines. It may be in any metre, but the most popular form in English poetry is the *heroic couplet* (iambic pentameter) which was first used by Chaucer.

Deus ex machina. Originally the term meant a god lowered on to the stage by machinery, who would intervene in the dramatic action. Nowadays it often means a rather far-fetched device for bringing about a resolution of the plot.

Dramatic monologue. This is a poetic and not really a dramatic form, in which one character is addressing an audience (perhaps of only one other person) and thus reveals his thoughts, motives, desires, etc. It was exploited by Victorian poets and especially by Browning, who made brilliant use of it in poems such as *Bishop Blougram's Apology*, *Fra Lippo Lippi*, *Andrea del Sarto*, etc.

Eclogue. See **Pastoral.**

Elegy. Originally the elegy was any classical poem written in elegiac verse, generally pentameters, and with a meditative subject, but in English poetry it has come to mean a lamentation for a dead person. It has often included religious and moral reflections as much as personal grief, *e.g.* Gray's *Elegy in a Country Churchyard* and Hopkins's *The Wreck of the Deutschland*. The *pastoral elegy* borrowed from classical tradition by representing the mourner and the mourned as fellow shepherds. This form, too, includes more than lamentation and, as in Milton's *Lycidas* (the finest example in English), introduces subjects such as divine justice and the corruption of contemporary society. (*v.* **Pastoral.**)

Enjambement. A French word which signifies the running-on of the sense beyond the end of a line of verse. It is used especially of the couplet in which the sentence is left unfinished at the completion of the second line. The opposite of enjambement is the *end-stopped line*.

Epigram. Originally the epigram was a short poem—especially a couplet or quatrain—which expressed a witty or pithy thought, *e.g.* the lines written by Pope for inscription on the collar of the Prince of Wales's dog,

> I am his Highness' dog at Kew;
> Pray tell me, sir, whose dog are you?

Later the term was also used of a short passage of a similar kind incorporated into a longer poem, *e.g.* Pope's

> Triumphant Leaders at an Army's head,
> Hemm'd round with Glories, pilfer Cloth or Bread,
> As meanly plunder as they bravely fought,
> Now save a People, and now save a Groat.

Today it can mean any witty saying, *e.g.* Oscar Wilde's

> 'Work is the curse of the drinking classes'.

Epithalamion (sometimes spelt **Epithalamium**) is a poem written in celebration of a marriage. The best-known example in English is Spenser's *Epithalamion*, which he wrote for his own bride.

Epode. See **Antistrophe** and **Ode.**

Euphuism is taken from Lyly's prose romance *Euphues* (1579). It is the name for the highly ornate and artificial style used by Lyly or for a style modelled on his.

Folio. In producing a book the printer first prints the pages on large sheets of paper which are then folded and bound together. If the book is a folio the sheets contain only two pages of print on each side and the sheet is folded once before binding. In a *quarto* four pages are printed on each side of the sheet and it is folded twice. In an *octavo* the sheet has eight pages on each side and is folded three times before binding; in a *duodecimo* it has twelve pages on each side and is folded four times. The more pages are printed on a single sheet and the more times it is folded, the smaller the book becomes. Hence a folio is a very large volume and the others named are in descending order of size. Some of Shakespeare's plays were first published separately in quarto; they were gathered together for the first time in 1623, in one volume, in what we call the First Folio edition. (*v.* R. B. McKerrow, *An Introduction to Bibliography*, 1927.)

Free Verse is verse composed without any regular metrical pattern but with more rhythm than ordinary speech. The French equivalent, *vers libre*, is sometimes used for this term.

Genre is a French term for 'form' or 'kind'. The main literary *genres* are discussed in Chapter Two and the minor ones such as elegy, lyric, etc. are included in this Glossary.

Gothic Novel. The Gothic novel, or Novel of Terror as it is sometimes called, became popular in the eighteenth century with the appearance of Horace Walpole's *Castle of Otranto*. It was part of the cult of medievalism which grew as the century moved towards Romanticism. The Gothic novel was generally set in an ancient castle or abbey and made ample use of devices such as sliding panels, ghosts, dungeons, etc. Jane Austen parodied the form in *Northanger Abbey*. (*v.* Edith Birkhead, *The Tale of Terror*, 1921.)

Humour. Today the word means something that causes amusement. This use derives from the humorous characters of the Elizabethan drama. But 'humour' in the Elizabethan period was a physiological term. There were thought to be four humours or fluids in the human body and a preponderance of any one of them produced one of four different types of personality. The humours were blood (hence the sanguinary man), phlegm (the phlegmatic man), choler, literally 'bile' (the choleric man), and melancholy, literally 'black bile' (the melancholy man). This physiological and psychological theory led Ben Jonson to develop his *comedy of humours*, in which the chief characters are often examples of these idiosyncratic types.

Hyperbole. A highly exaggerated statement not meant to be taken literally.

Idyll. See **Pastoral.**

Lyric. In ancient Greece the lyric was a song accompanied on the lyre. In English literature the term applies to any short poem which expresses feeling. The sixteenth and seventeenth centuries were the great periods of lyric poetry in England. (*v.* Norman Ault, *Elizabethan Lyrics*, 1925, *Seventeenth Century Lyrics*, 1928, and Catherine Ing, *Elizabethan Lyrics*, 1951.)

Masque. A form of dramatic entertainment which included poetry, music, song, dances and spectacle. The masque was a popular form in the Elizabethan period and early seventeenth century. It was generally produced at court or in one of the great houses of the nobility. The name derives from the dance of masked figures with which the performance ended. The best known masque is Milton's *Comus*, which was first presented at Ludlow Castle in 1634, but Milton's work is more serious and makes much less use of spectacle than the typical masque. (*v.* Enid Welsford, *The Court Masque*, 1927.)

Miracle and Morality Plays were medieval verse dramas. The miracle play represented episodes from the Bible or the lives of the saints. This kind of drama developed into cycles which covered the whole of sacred history from the Creation to the Last Judgement. Four of these cycles remain and have been edited from the original manuscripts. Three belong to York, Chester and Wakefield, while the fourth is unlocalized. The York cycle in a modern version is still performed at the York Festival. These plays are sometimes called *mystery plays* because they were acted by the various medieval crafts or guilds (Middle English *misterie*—trade) of the town. The *morality play* was a religious allegory in which the main characters were often personifications of virtues and vices. The most famous morality play is the fifteenth-century *Everyman*. (*v.* A. W. Pollard,

English Miracle Plays, Moralities and Interludes, 1923; Glynne Wickham, *Early English Stages, 1300–1660,* vol. I, 1959.)

Octave. See **Sonnet.**

Octavo. See **Folio.**

Ode. Originally in Greece the ode was a poem which was sung, especially by the chorus as part of a play. In English the ode is generally a long lyrical poem, often addressed to a person or to celebrate some occasion, and containing an element of reflection which is lacking in the pure lyric. The style varies from the exalted to the simple and familiar. The subject and the occasion show a wide variety. Milton composed an ode to celebrate Christ's nativity; Dryden wrote an ode to music (*Alexander's Feast*), and an ode to *Mistress Anne Killigrew*; Keats wrote his famous ode *To Autumn,* and Wordsworth the equally famous *Intimations of Immortality*; Coleridge called his poem *Dejection* an *Ode*; Tennyson composed an ode *On the Death of Wellington.* There is no established metrical pattern for the ode, the stanza is generally long with varying line lengths and rhymes; in the so-called *Horatian Ode,* however, there is a regular stanza form and here the subject-matter is less solemn (*e.g.* Marvell's *Horatian Ode upon Cromwell's Return from Ireland*). Another form is the *Pindaric Ode* which took as its model the odes of the Greek poet, Pindar, who adopted the choric pattern of strophe, antistrophe and epode (*v.* **Antistrophe**) from Greek drama. Cowley wrote irregular Pindaric odes in the seventeenth century, but in the next century a number of poets, especially Gray, wrote in direct imitation of Pindar, with the strophes and antistrophes in one stanza form, the epodes in another. Gray's *The Progress of Poesy* and *The Bard* are examples of the form. (*v.* E. Gosse, *English Odes,* 1881, and R. Shafer, *The English Ode to 1660,* 1918.)

Ottava Rima is a stanza of eight lines rhyming *abababcc.* It was introduced into English poetry from the Italian in the sixteenth century by Sir Thomas Wyatt. Byron exploited the comic and narrative potentialities of this stanza form in his *Don Juan.*

Pastoral. The word literally means 'concerning shepherds' and the Greek poet, Theocritus, started the convention of pastoral poetry in his *Idylls,* written in the third century B.C., but it was Vergil's *Eclogues* which gave the form its importance. Vergil, of course, lived in an urban society and his poems spring from the townsman's dream of a golden age in which men minded their flocks in peace and simplicity. The Elizabethans used the pastoral form as a vehicle for satire and the allegorization of contemporary questions, as in Spenser's *Shepheard's Calendar* (1579). There were also pastoral romances in prose, *e.g.* Sidney's *Arcadia.* The *pastoral elegy* (*v.* **Elegy**) combined pastoralism with lamentation by depicting shepherds mourning the death of one of their fellows. (*v.* W. W. Greg, *Pastoral Poetry and Pastoral Drama*, 1906, P. V. Marinelli, *Pastoral*, 1971.)

Protagonist. Another name for the hero or chief character in a story, especially in drama.

Quarto. See **Folio.**

Quatrain. A stanza of four lines of verse, usually with alternate rhymes.

Rhyme Royal is a seven-line stanza in iambic pentameters, rhyming *ababbcc*. It was first used in English by Chaucer in *Troilus and Criseyde*, etc.

Satire is a composition in verse or prose that ridicules a subject, especially the vices of an individual or a society. Comedy in some of its forms comes very close to satire, but differs in its pure form because satire uses laughter as a means to an end and not for itself. The great age of English satire was the eighteenth century. (*v.* Ian Jack, *Augustan Satire*, 1952, and J. D. Peter, *Complaint and Satire in early English Literature*, 1956.

Sestet. See **Sonnet.**

Sonnet is a lyric poem of fourteen lines. There are two forms of the sonnet. The *Petrarchan sonnet* is divided into two parts: an *octave* (8 lines) rhyming *abbaabba* and a *sestet* (6 lines) rhyming *cdecde*. Sir Thomas Wyatt introduced this form into England in the early sixteenth century. The *Shakespearian sonnet* is divided into three quatrains rhyming *abab*, *cdcd*, *efef*, and a final couplet rhyming *gg*.

Spenserian Stanza was invented by Spenser and used in *The Faerie Queene*. There are nine lines in the Spenserian Stanza, the first eight are iambic pentameters and the last is an iambic hexameter (*v.* **Alexandrine**). The rhyme scheme is *ababbcbcc*. It is an ample and leisurely unit suited to the long narrative poem. Some eighteenth-century poets, such as James Thomson (*The Castle of Indolence*), wrote in this stanza form in conscious imitation of Spenser, and it was also adopted by Keats in his *Eve of St Agnes* and by Shelley in *Adonais*.

Strophe. See **Antistrophe** and **Ode.**

Terza Rima is an Italian form of stanza which Dante used in his *Divine Comedy*. It was used by Sir Thomas Wyatt in the early sixteenth century after his visit to Italy, but Chaucer had already experimented with it in the *Complaint to his Lady*. In *terza rima* the stanzas are tercets, but linked together by a running rhyme as follows, *aba*, *bcb*, *cdc*, *ded*, etc. It is not very common in English, but good examples are Browning's *The Statue and the Bust* and Shelley's *Ode to the West Wind*.

The Wreck of the Deutschland
by Gerard Manley Hopkins

To the
happy memory of five Franciscan Nuns
exiles by the Falk[1] Laws
drowned between midnight and morning of
Dec. 7th, 1875

PART THE FIRST

1

Thou mastering me
God! giver of breath and bread;
World's strand, sway of the sea;
Lord of living and dead;
Thou hast bound bones and veins in me, fastened me flesh,
And after it almost unmade, what with dread,
Thy doing: and dost thou touch me afresh?
Over again I feel thy finger and find thee.

2

I did say yes
O at lightning and lashed rod;
Thou heardst me truer than tongue confess
Thy terror, O Christ, O God;
Thou knowest the walls, altar and hour and night:
The swoon of a heart that the sweep and the hurl of thee trod
Hard down with a horror of height:
And the midriff astrain with leaning of, laced with fire of stress.

[1] Dr Falk was Minister of Education in Germany under Bismark and helped to frame the laws which brought the Roman Catholic Church under State control in that country.

3

The frown of his face
Before me, the hurtle of hell
Behind, where, where was a, where was a place?
I whirled out wings that spell
And fled with a fling of the heart to the heart of the Host.
My heart, but you were dovewinged, I can tell,
Carrier-witted, I am bold to boast,
To flash from the flame to the flame then, tower from the grace to the
grace.

4

I am soft sift
In an hourglass—at the wall
Fast, but mined with a motion, a drift,
And it crowds and it combs to the fall;
I steady as a water in a well, to a poise, to a pane,
But roped with, always, all the way down from the tall
Fells or flanks of the voel, a vein
Of the gospel proffer, a pressure, a principle, Christ's gift.

5

I kiss my hand
To the stars, lovely-asunder
Starlight, wafting him out of it; and
Glow, glory in thunder;
Kiss my hand to the dappled-with-damson west:
Since, tho' he is under the world's splendour and wonder,
His mystery must be instressed, stressed;
For I greet him the days I meet him, and bless when I understand.

6

Not out of his bliss
Springs the stress felt
Nor first from heaven (and few know this)
Swings the stroke dealt—
Stroke and a stress that stars and storms deliver,
That guilt is hushed by, hearts are flushed by and melt—
But it rides time like riding a river
(And here the faithful waver, the faithless fable and miss).

7

It dates from day
Of his going in Galilee;
Warm-laid grave of a womb-life grey;
Manger, maiden's knee;
The dense and the driven Passion, and frightful sweat;
Thence the discharge of it, there its swelling to be,
Though felt before, though in high flood yet—
What none would have known of it, only the heart, being hard at bay,

8

Is out with it! Oh,
We lash with the best or worst.
Word last! How a lush-kept plush-capped sloe
Will, mouthed to flesh-burst,
Gush!—flush the man, the being with it, sour or sweet,
Brim, in a flash, full!—Hither then, last or first,
To hero of Calvary, Christ's feet—
Never ask if meaning it, wanting it, warned of it—men go.

9

Be adored among men,
God, three-numberèd form;
Wring thy rebel, dogged in den,
Man's malice, with wrecking and storm.
Beyond saying sweet, past telling of tongue,
Thou art lightning and love, I found it, a winter and warm;
Father and fondler of heart thou hast wrung:
Hast thy dark descending and most art merciful then.

10

With an anvil-ding
And with fire in him forge thy will
Or rather, rather then, stealing as Spring
Through him, melt him but master him still:
Whether at once, as once at a crash Paul,
Or as Austin, a lingering-out sweet skill,
Make mercy in all of us, out of us all
Mastery, but be adored, but be adored King.

PART THE SECOND

11

'Some find me a sword; some
  The flange and the rail; flame,
Fang, or flood' goes Death on drum,
  And storms bugle his fame.
But wé dream we are rooted in earth—Dust!
  Flesh falls within sight of us, we, though our flower the same,
    Wave with the meadow, forget that there must
The sour scythe cringe, and the blear share come.

12

On Saturday sailed from Bremen,
  American-outward-bound,
Take settler and seamen, tell men with women,
  Two hundred souls in the round—
O Father, not under thy feathers nor ever as guessing
  The goal was a shoal, of a fourth the doom to be drowned;
    Yet did the dark side of the bay of thy blessing
Not vault them, the millions of rounds of thy mercy not reeve even them
  in?

13

Into the snows she sweeps,
  Hurling the haven behind,
The Deutschland, on Sunday; and so the sky keeps,
  For the infinite air is unkind,
And the sea flint-flake, black-backed in the regular blow,
  Sitting Eastnortheast, in cursed quarter, the wind;
    Wiry and white-fiery and whirlwind-swivellèd snow
Spins to the widow-making unchilding unfathering deeps.

14

She drove in the dark to leeward,
  She struck—not a reef or a rock
But the combs of a smother of sand: night drew her
  Dead to the Kentish Knock;
And she beat the bank down with her bows and the ride of her keel:
  The breakers rolled on her beam with ruinous shock;
    And canvas and compass, the whorl and the wheel
Idle for ever to waft her or wind her with, these she endured.

15

Hope had grown grey hairs,
Hope had mourning on,
Trenched with tears, carved with cares,
Hope was twelve hours gone;
And frightful a nightfall folded rueful a day
Nor rescue, only rocket and lightship, shone,
And lives at last were washing away:
To the shrouds they took,—they shook in the hurling and horrible airs.

16

One stirred from the rigging to save
The wild woman-kind below,
With a rope's end round the man, handy and brave—
He was pitched to his death at a blow,
For all his dreadnought breast and braids of thew:
They could tell him for hours, dandled the to and fro
Through the cobbled foam-fleece, what could he do
With the burl of the fountains of air, buck and the flood of the wave?

17

They fought with God's cold—
And they could not and fell to the deck
(Crushed them) or water (and drowned them) or rolled
With the sea-romp over the wreck.
Night roared, with the heart-break hearing a heart-broke rabble,
The woman's wailing, the crying of child without check—
Till a lioness arose breasting the babble,
A prophetess towered in the tumult, a virginal tongue told.

18

Ah, touched in your bower of bone
Are you! turned for an exquisite smart,
Have you! make words break from me here all alone,
Do you!—mother of being in me, heart.
O unteachably after evil, but uttering truth,
Why, tears! is it? tears; such a melting, a madrigal start!
Never-eldering revel and river of youth,
What can it be, this glee? the good you have there of your own?

19

Sister, a sister calling
A master, her master and mine!—

And the inboard seas run swirling and hawling;
    The rash smart sloggering brine
Blinds her; but she that weather sees one thing, one;
    Has one fetch in her: she rears herself to divine
Ears, and the call of the tall nun
To the men in the tops and the tackle rode over the storm's brawling.

20

    She was first of a five and came
    Of a coifèd sisterhood.
    (O Deutschland, double a desperate name!
    O world wide of its good!
But Gertrude, lily, and Luther, are two of a town,
    Christ's lily and beast of the waste wood:
    From life's dawn it is drawn down,
Abel is Cain's brother and breasts they have sucked the same.)

21

    Loathed for a love men knew in them,
    Banned by the land of their birth,
    Rhine refused them. Thames would ruin them;
    Surf, snow, river and earth
Gnashed: but thou art above, thou Orion of light;
    Thy unchancelling posing palms were weighing the worth,
    Thou martyr-master: in thy sight
Storm flakes were scroll-leaved flowers, lily showers—sweet heaven was
astrew in them.

22

    Five! the finding and sake
    And cipher of suffering Christ.
    Mark, the mark is of man's make
    And the word of it Sacrificed.
But he scores it in scarlet himself on his own bespoken,
    Before-time-taken, dearest prizèd and priced—
    Stigma, signal, cinquefoil token
For lettering of the lamb's fleece, ruddying of the rose-flake.

23

    Joy fall to thee, father Francis,
    Drawn to the Life that died;

With the gnarls of the nails in thee, niche of the lance, his
    Lovescape crucified
And seal of his seraph-arrival! and these thy daughters
    And five-livèd and leavèd favour and pride,
      Are sisterly sealed in wild waters,
To bathe in his fall-gold mercies, to breathe in his all-fire glances.

24

    Away in the loveable west,
      On a pastoral forehead of Wales,
    I was under a roof here, I was at rest,
      And they the prey of the gales;
  She to the black-about air, to the breaker, the thickly
  Falling flakes, to the throng that catches and· quails
    Was calling 'O Christ, Christ, come quickly':
The cross to her she calls Christ to her, christens her wild-worst Best.

25

    The majesty! what did she mean?
      Breathe, arch and original Breath.
  Is it love in her of the being as her lover had been?
      Breathe, body of lovely Death.
  They were else-minded then, altogether, the men
Woke thee with a *we are perishing* in the weather of Gennesareth.
    Or is it that she cried for the crown then,
The keener to come at the comfort for feeling the combating keen?

26

    For how to the heart's cheering
      The down-dugged ground-hugged grey
  Hovers off, the jay-blue heavens appearing
      Of pied and peeled May!
  Blue-beating and hoary-glow height; or night, still higher,
  With belled fire and the moth-soft Milky Way,
    What by your measure is the heaven of desire,
The treasure never eyesight got, nor was ever guessed what for the
    hearing?

27

    No, but it was not these.
      The jading and jar of the cart,
  Time's tasking, it is fathers that asking for ease

Of the sodden-with-its-sorrowing heart,
Not danger, electrical horror; then further it finds
The appealing of the Passion is tenderer in prayer apart:
Other, I gather, in measure her mind's
Burden, in wind's burly and beat of endragonèd seas.

28

But how shall I . . . make me room there:
Reach me a . . . Fancy, come faster—
Strike you the sight of it? look at it loom there,
Thing that she . . . there then! the Master,
Ipse, the only one, Christ, King, Head:
He was to cure the extremity where he had cast her;
Do, deal, lord it with living and dead;
Let him ride, her pride, in his triumph, despatch and have done with his
doom there.

29

Ah! there was a heart right!
There was single eye!
Read the unshapeable shock night
And knew the who and the why;
Wording it how but by him that present and past,
Heaven and earth are word of, worded by?—
The Simon Peter of a soul! to the blast
Tarpeian-fast, but a blown beacon of light.

30

Jesu, heart's light,
Jesu, maid's son,
What was the feast followed the night
Thou hadst glory of this nun?—
Feast of the one woman without stain.
For so conceivèd, so to conceive thee is done;
But here was heart-throe, birth of a brain,
Word, that heard and kept thee and uttered thee outright.

31

Well, she has thee for the pain, for the
Patience; but pity of the rest of them!
Heart, go and bleed at a bitterer vein for the
Comfortless unconfessed of them—

No not uncomforted: lovely-felicitous Providence
Finger of a tender of, O of a feathery delicacy, the breast of the
  Maiden could obey so, be a bell to, ring of it, and
Startle the poor sheep back! is the shipwrack then a harvest, does tempest
carry the grain for thee?

32

I admire thee, master of the tides,
  Of the Yore-flood, of the year's fall;
The recurb and the recovery of the gulf's sides,
  The girth of it and the wharf of it and the wall;
Stanching, quenching ocean of a motionable mind;
  Ground of being, and granite of it: past all
   Grasp God, throned behind
Death with a sovereignty that heeds but hides, bodes but abides;

33

With a mercy that outrides
  The all of water, an ark
For the listener; for the lingerer with a love glides
  Lower than death and the dark;
A vein for the visiting of the past-prayer, pent in prison,
  The last-breath penitent spirits—the uttermost mark
   Our passion-plungèd giant risen,
The Christ of the Father compassionate, fetched in the storm of his
strides.

34

Now burn, new born to the world,
  Doubled-naturèd name
The heaven-flung, heart-fleshed, maiden-furled
  Miracle-in-Mary-of-flame,
Mid-numbered He in three of the thunder-throne!
  Not a dooms-day dazzle in his coming nor dark as he came;
   Kind, but royally reclaiming his own;
A released shower, let flash to the shire, not a lightning of fire hard-
hurled.

35

Dame, at our door
  Drowned, and among our shoals,
Remember us in the roads, the heaven-haven of the Reward:

Our King back, oh, upon English souls!
Let him easter in us, be a dayspring to the dimness of us, be a crim-
    son-cresseted east,
More brightening her, rare-dear Britain, as his reign rolls,
    Pride, rose, prince, hero of us, high-priest,
Our hearts' charity's hearth's fire, our thoughts' chivalry's throng's Lord.

Index

Absurd, Theatre of the: 18
Accent: 48–50
Alexandrine: 70
Allegory: 28–9
Alliteration: 45–6
Anagnorisis (recognition): 14
Anapaest: 50, 52
Antistrophe: 70
Apostrophe: 70
Archetypal Images: 30–1
Assonance: 46–7

Ballad: 70
Blank Verse: 51

Caesura: 35, 36, 45
Catachresis: 26
Chiasmus: 36
Chorus: 70
Comedy: 16–18
Comedy of Humours: 73
Comedy of Manners: 17
Conceit: 24–5
Consonance: 47
Couplet: 35, 36, 53, 71
Criticism (Literary): Ch. 8

Dactyl: 50, 52
Deus ex machina: 71
Dramatic Irony: 39
Dramatic Monologue: 71
Duodecimo: *See* Folio

Eclogue: *See* Pastoral
Elegy: 71
Enjambement: 71

Epic: 8–10
Epigram: 71–2
Epithalamion: 72
Epode: *See* Antistrophe
Euphuism: 72

Figures of Meaning: 1–2, Chs. 3
    and 4
Figures of Sound: Ch. 5
Folio: 72
Free Verse: 72

Genres (Literary): Ch. 2
Gothic Novel: 72

Hamartia (tragic flaw): 13
Heroic Couplet: 71
Heroic Drama: 16
Horatian Ode: 74
Hubris (pride): 13
Humour: 73
Hyperbole: 73

Iambus: 50, 51
Idyll: *See* Pastoral
Image: 22–4
Imitation: 12, 64
Irony: 39–41

Katharsis (purgation): 13, 18, 64

Language: Ch. 1, Ch. 7, 68–9
Literary Criticism: Ch. 8
Lyric: 73

Masque: 73
Metaphor: 2, 24–6

Metaphysical Conceit: 24–5
Metonym: 23, 29
Metre: Ch. 6
Mimesis (imitation): 12, 64
Miracle Plays: 73
Mock Epic: 11, 39–40
Monologue (Dramatic): 71
Morality Plays: 73
Muthos (plot): 14
Mystery Plays: 71
Myth: 32–4

Nemesis: 13, 18
Nonsense Verse: 42
Novel, The: 19–20, (Gothic) 72

Octave: *See* Sonnet
Octavo: *See* Folio
Ode: 74
Onomatopoeia: 43
Ottava Rima: 74
Oxymoron: 36, 38

Paradox: 37–9
Pastoral: 74
Peripeteia (reversal): 13
Personification: 26–8
Pindaric Ode: 74
Plot: 14
Pride: 13
Prosody: Ch. 6
Purgation: 13, 18, 64
Pyrrhic: 50

Quantity: 50–6
Quarto: *See* Folio
Quatrain: 53, 75

Recognition: 14
Revenge Plays: 15
Reversal: 13, 15
Rhetoric: 2
Rhyme: 44–5
Rhyme Royal: 75
Ridicule: 11, 18

Satire: 11, 40, 75
Senecan Tragedy: 15
Sestet: *See* Sonnet
Simile: 2, 24–6
Sonnet: 75
Spenserian: Stanza: 75
Spondee: 50
Sprung Rhythm: 54–5
Stress: 48–50
Strophe: *See* Antistrophe
Structuralism: 68–9
Style: Ch. 7
Stylistics: 68–9
Symbol: 28–32

Tercet: 53
Terza Rima: 75
Tragedy: 11–16
Tragic Flaw: 13
Tragi-comedy: 15–16
Trochee: 50, 51
Tropes: 1, 22, 35

Unities: 12–13

Vers Libre: *See* Free Verse

Zeugma: 36